Hip Sips

# Hip Sips

Modern
Cocktails
to
Raise
Your
Spirits

by **Lucy Brennan** with Carolyn Burleigh

Photographs by **Sheri Giblin**

**CHRONICLE BOOKS**

SAN FRANCISCO

## Acknowledgments

Since I almost never became a bartender, thanks to Joe "Tecate and Jager" for seeing my future without me even knowing it. Thanks to Debra Curtis, who suggested to Bruce Carey and Chris Israel that they hire me for the Christmas party, and again to Bruce and Chris for giving me creative freedom with the cocktail list at Saucebox. To Marco Dionysus, cheers for teaching me all you know about making drinks and for endless late nights talking about cocktails. I've trained a lot of bartenders in my day, and two stand out as the best: Greg "Just Kidding" Martin and Rebecca Steele, thank you both for helping me with my ongoing cocktail list at Mint and 820 and with this book. Ryan Magarian, thank you for your friendship and love for life and cocktails. Carolyn Burleigh, this book would not have been possible without you—thank you, you rock! Melissa Broussard, thank you for your support and drive to get this book published. Mona Cordell and Sue Davis, thank you for your support and smiles. Charmaine Shively, since day one you have been a supporter of my cocktails and were never afraid to let me know when one needed work. Your love and strong will have kept me on track over the years and made this book possible. I thank you and know there aren't enough words to let you know how much. Last, but not least, many thanks to my family and friends for many years of love.

**—Lucy Brennan**

Thanks to Mom, Dad, and Gordon, for their love and support. To Diane Morgan, thanks for generously sharing your experience and knowledge of cookbook writing. To Lucy Brennan, thanks for teaching me how to make a great drink and for partnering with me on this project. And thanks to Geri Laufer, who wouldn't let me stop writing query letters until I published my first article.

**—Carolyn Burleigh**

Library of Congress Cataloging-in-Publication Data available.

ISBN-10 0-8118-4958-9
ISBN-13 978-0-8118-4958-6

Manufactured in China.

Food and prop styling by **Spork**
Designed by **Vanessa Dina**
Typesetting by **Janis Reed**

Distributed in Canada
by Raincoast Books
9050 Shaughnessy Street
Vancouver, BC V6P 6E5

10 9 8 7 6 5 4 3 2 1

Chronicle Books LLC
680 Second Street
San Francisco, CA 94107

www.chroniclebooks.com

Dedication

This book is dedicated to my boy Charlie—
I miss your baggy trousers!

# Contents

**Introduction 9**

# Introduction

Before I'll invite anyone to dinner, I'll invite them for cocktails. It's not that I don't like to cook. It's that everything I've ever learned about making a great meal, I've translated into the creativity that I use to invent cocktails.

Where chefs use a flame, I use ice. Instead of copper pots, I prefer a stainless-steel cocktail shaker. For a mortar and pestle, I substitute a five-dollar muddler and a tempered pint glass. My modified whisking technique is a quick above-the-shoulder motion that could prime the forearms of any major league pitcher. The resulting liquid bliss is my take on cold fusion, which unites the flavors of fresh ingredients, distilled spirits, and artisan liqueurs and thrives in a 10-ounce martini glass.

*Hip Sips* is a collection of food-forward cocktails that were introduced to the public at my first restaurant, Mint, in Portland, Oregon. Before opening Mint, I was gaining a reputation as one of the best bartenders in the city for my specialty drinks with out-of-the-ordinary ingredients, and I knew that my fruit-, vegetable-, and herb-laden cocktails needed their own home.

In many restaurants, the bar and the kitchen are separate units that come together only long enough for the quick hand-off of lemon wedges. When I opened Mint, I made sure to remove that invisible barrier and make room for the next generation of cocktails.

When you visit Mint or the lounge next door, 820, you will see a wooden bowl, prominently placed on the bar, filled with avocados, oranges, lemons, and limes. These ingredients are just a hint of what goes on behind the bar and in my experiments marrying culinary arts and mixology.

The cocktails in this book differ from traditional mixed drinks because they use ingredients more often found in the produce aisles of grocery stores than behind smoke-filled bars. What makes these sips hip is the use of such food-forward ingredients as fresh fruit juices and purées, homemade vegetable- or fruit-infused vodkas, and fresh herbs. These components are easily prepared and make all the difference in the flavor of the drinks. The ingredients are chosen to complement each other, not to disguise the taste of the alcohol. Each drink relies on spirits as catalysts and a vigorous ten-second shake to combine the ingredients.

With the lines between kitchen and bar blurred, and relying on the age-old methods of muddling and infusing, these modern-day cocktails have a place at the table as insightful pairings with multi-course meals, or on their own as a novel way to enjoy the flavors of seasonal ingredients.

*Hip Sips* begins with an introduction to the essentials of stocking a home bar and insights into the fundamentals of making a great cocktail. The next four chapters are filled with recipes for modern, inventive mixed drinks. The cocktails you'll find in "Fruit Escapes" inspire a quick good-bye to the Greyhound and a hello to the Guava Cosmo. Vodka, gin, tequila, and rum are freed from the prerequisite splash of juice or soda and energized with high-quality fruit purées and sugared lollipop rims.

"Brave New World" is the chapter where food-forward cocktails come into full bloom with recipes for Beet-Infused Vodka and Avocado Daiquiris. These cocktails are exceptional examples of avant-garde mixology and explore exotic combinations of food and spirits.

A cocktail book would not be complete without at least a handful of standards that will have you lacing up your wingtips and singing Sinatra. "Sentimental Sips" includes recipes for traditional favorites, and in "Lucy's Twists" you'll find a few new interpretations that re-create old stand-bys with signature touches of food infusion. The "Mocktails" chapter presents nonalcoholic mixed drinks that have the same amount of verve and flavor as spirit-infused concoctions.

*Hip Sips* mixologists imagine new drinks daily and are likely to be found shopping Saturday's farmers' market for the freshest cocktail ingredients. After tasting a few of these food-forward cocktails, I think you'll understand how it can be as inspiring to make a four-ounce drink as it is a four-course meal.

# Hip Sips 101

## Glassware

**10-ounce martini glass:** A stemware basic for many of the *Hip Sips* cocktails. The oversized cup is excellent for serving decadent drinks that demand an impressive presentation. The wide-mouthed lip leaves enough room for a lavish lollipop rim without overwhelming the glass.

**5-ounce martini glass:** The customary size for traditional martini-style drinks. Rather than chilling this glass in the freezer, which leaves the stem cold and wet, quickly chill it while making the cocktail by adding ice and water.

**Bucket (or double old-fashioned) glass:** A 10-ounce bucket glass is the popular choice for margarita-style drinks or drinks that are shaken and then poured on the rocks.

**Collins glass:** A tall 12-ounce Collins glass is recommended for mixed drinks with additional carbonation from Champagne or soda water.

**Balloon wineglass:** This 12-ounce goblet-style stemware gives a festive touch to daiquiris and is also a glamorous alternative for serving margaritas.

**Heat-resistant wineglass:** Consider serving steaming-hot cocktails in a 12-ounce heat-resistant wineglass. This tall, tulip-shaped glass is simply the generic, inexpensive kind made with thicker glass (not crystal), found in hardware stores or restaurant supply houses. Your local kitchen store can also help you find them. This stemware adds a sophisticated touch to hot drinks.

**Footed coffee mug:** A 10-ounce clear-glass footed coffee mug is best for traditional Irish coffees.

**Pint glass:** Used for my Irish Stout Sangría and mocktails.

# Tools

The objects needed to create a *Hip Sips* cocktail are few. Your imagination and these basic tools are all you need to mix a drink. What makes a successful drink is not the latest designer cocktail shaker, but quality ingredients and a powerful shake. That's it. In fact, most of these items are available at your favorite kitchen supply store or even the local Cash and Carry, where under the harsh glare of fluorescent lighting, you can stock up on a year's supply of dish detergent and your essential bar tools.

**Tempered pint glass:** Almost every *Hip Sips* cocktail begins with a pint glass packed full with ice cubes. A tempered 16-ounce pint glass is an essential tool for chilling ingredients before shaking the drink and also takes the place of a mortar when muddling ingredients. The tempered glass is sturdy enough to withstand a hearty muddling with ice without breaking.

**Stainless-steel cocktail shaker:** Reminiscent of an ice cream parlor milkshake container, this wide-mouthed 30-ounce stainless-steel cup fits easily on top of a pint glass and, except for a little muscle, is all you need to successfully shake up a cocktail.

**Muddler:** With a pint glass as your mortar, a muddler becomes your pestle. For making cocktails, it is best to choose a lightweight wooden muddler with a smooth, rounded surface on the end.

**Measured shot glass:** Since the majority of cocktails require various amounts of spirits, having a shot glass with ounces marked on the outside makes mixing drinks a simple process.

**Bar spoon:** A 12-inch stainless-steel swiveled bar spoon is invaluable for carefully stirring a drink.

**Vegetable peeler:** Food-forward drinks call for generous citrus zests. A standard vegetable peeler ensures no wimpy twists for your cocktail.

# Ice: The Agitator

Ice is not just about keeping things chilled. It is the agent of change, agitating ingredients in a cocktail shaker to create something new.

**Note: Size matters.** *Hip Sips* cocktails get their start in a pint glass full of cocktail ice cubes. Most likely the ice cubes from your refrigerator are too big. Choose $1/2$-inch cubes, which are small enough to mix it up inside the confines of a pint glass. You can purchase smaller size ice cubes (not crushed ice) from the grocery store, and buying bags of ice will also ensure that you have plenty of ice for your party.

From shaking to sandwiching to muddling, ice releases and unites flavors.

**Shaking:** Shaking agitates individual components and aids in blending the mix.

**Sandwiching:** Sandwiching wakes up sleeping herbs to diffuse their flavors throughout the drink. Sandwiching is most often used with delicate herbs such as mint. Muddling mint, by contrast, overworks the herb and adds a strong, almost bitter aftertaste to a mixed drink.

To sandwich a fresh herb, add about $1/2$ cup of ice to the pint glass. Add the herb leaves next. Cover with enough ice to fill the glass. Shake the glass to bruise each leaf and release the essence of the herb.

**Muddling:** During muddling, the ice helps to macerate each component and create a flavorful slush that readily mixes with other ingredients. Muddling is necessary to completely release the powerful flavors of such ingredients as lemons, cherries, or cilantro.

To begin muddling, first add about $1/2$ cup of cocktail ice cubes to your pint glass, then top with the recipe's fresh ingredients such as lemon wedges. Using a lightweight wooden muddler, crush the ice and fruit until the ice is slushy and colorful and the fruit is completely macerated. Add ice to fill the pint glass and add the remainder of the drink ingredients. Shake and serve.

**On the rocks:** If a cocktail is being served on the rocks, pour the same ice used to mix the drink into the glass. Cocktails get an extra flavor boost when ice from the cocktail shaker is poured directly into the drink.

Remember, ice is the workhorse in drink making. So, get shaking, and never take ice for granted.

# How to Stock the Bar

Of course, one of the most important elements in a cocktail is the alcohol, but with so many choices it can be a daunting task to stock a home bar. Spirits have greatly evolved over the years as more and more producers advance the craft, fine-tuning distillation methods and introducing new ingredients to top-shelf liquors. Connoisseurs of prize liquors are similar to wine aficionados and can pick out flavor nuances that reflect how each spirit was created.

Because stocking a home bar is an investment, *Hip Sips* has two solutions for equipping a liquor cabinet. The Downtown Bar is a basic collection of spirits that are most often used for well drinks in bars. These spirits are extremely compatible ingredients in cocktails and can also be enjoyed straight up.

The Uptown Bar is a collection of exceptional, high-end spirits. Producers maintain a higher attention to detail in the distillation process for these top-shelf spirits, which results in distinctive, smooth flavors. Any of them can be served neat to savor each sip or be a part of a top-drawer mixed drink.

## The Downtown Bar

**Maker's Mark bourbon:** This agreeable bourbon adds slightly sweet flavors of nuts, coffee, and caramel to a Manhattan, a whiskey sour, or a Mandarin Kiss.

**Korbel brandy:** A light brandy distilled from grapes and aged in oak.

**Cascade Mountain gin:** A domestic gin from Bend, Oregon, crafted with hand-picked fresh juniper. The slightly sweet, light citrus taste can stand straight up in a martini and is a welcome addition to gin-based cocktails. If you have trouble finding Cascade Mountain gin, Tanqueray can be substituted.

**Harlequin orange liqueur:** This French liqueur is a common ingredient in many *Hip Sips* cocktails. Preferred over Grand Marnier because of its light flavor, Harlequin adds structure without overpowering other drink ingredients.

**Barbancourt Three Star rum:** Aged for four years in oak barrels, this Haitian rum has a slightly floral nose, with soft undertones of dried apricots.

**Sauza Hornitos tequila:** A gold tequila made from 100 percent agave and aged in new American white oak barrels. An excellent household tequila for margaritas, with hints of salt, apples, pears, and a momentary kick of black pepper.

**Monopolowa vodka:** Monopolowa is potato vodka that has been made for over two hundred years. This mild yet distinctive vodka is ideal for making cocktails, as it has a clean flavor that doesn't compete with the other ingredients.

**Bushmills Irish whiskey:** Aged a minimum of five years in oak casks and then blended with a single-malt whiskey, Bushmills is a soothing sipping whiskey with no hint of peat.

**Dewar's Blended Scotch whisky:** Dewar's is a classic Scotch that should be a staple in any bar.

## The Uptown Bar

**Black Maple Hill 14-year-old bourbon:** This high-end, single-barrel bourbon comes in three aged varieties. The fourteen-year-old liquor has hints of oak, spice, wood, and a little caramel. The finish is dry and even a little sweet.

**Carlos I Spanish brandy:** This brandy features a soft nose of almonds and butterscotch, with notes of vanilla and nutmeg in the long finish.

**Boodles gin:** A classic martini gin, dry with hints of citrus and juniper and a smooth, oily finish.

**Hendrick's gin:** This Scottish gin embellishes an age-old spirit by including rose petals and cucumber in the distillation process.

**Cointreau orange liqueur:** A high-end orange Cognac that doesn't overwhelm other drink ingredients.

**Nocello liqueur:** It is easy to fall in love with this walnut liqueur, which can be savored by itself in place of dessert. Similar to but not as sweet as Frangelico, which is made with hazelnuts.

**Captain Morgan Private Stock spiced rum:** A high-end Puerto Rican rum that whispers of caramel and vanilla in the nose and taste. Its sweet, rich flavors can be sipped or enjoyed in mixed drinks.

**Pampero Anniversario rum:** A dark amber rum with a creamy texture; notes of walnut, oak, and vanilla in the nose; and a sweet allspice taste.

**Pyrat Pistol rum:** This sweet sipping rum is an elegant after-dinner selection.

**Glenmorangie Port Wood Finish 12-year-old single malt Scotch whisky:** Light and robust at the same time, this approachable single malt has memorable suggestions of port but no heat in the finish.

**Don Eduardo Añejo tequila:** A light sipping tequila, aged in American white oak bourbon barrels for two years.

**Don Eduardo Silver tequila:** This tequila is distilled three times with a nice bouquet of citrus and herbs. It's mild in taste with a short finish, and a little pepper comes through in each sip.

**Ciroc vodka:** An unusual French vodka made from white grapes distilled five times, Ciroc has a little bite and a slight heat. It is excellent well chilled, with a twist of lemon.

**Grey Goose vodka:** This premier spirit slinks across your palate with no residual heat.

**Grey Goose Le Citron vodka:** A penetrating vodka with a nonchalant citrus finish, this is an ideal choice when experimenting with the Original Lemon Drop (page 99).

**Grey Goose L'Orange vodka:** This vodka has a smooth, slight citrus finish.

**Hangar One vodka:** A domestic vodka, made from Viognier grapes, Hangar One has a scant sweetness and a touch of citrus, and is an exceptional choice for a traditional martini.

**Johnnie Walker Gold Label Scotch whisky:** This eighteen-year-old Scotch is a little creamy, with a long, silky finish. A best-kept secret is to serve it chilled and paired with chocolate truffles for dessert.

**The Macallan 18-year-old single sherry oak cask malt Highland Scotch whisky:** This complex whiskey has a little smoke and peat.

## More Essentials

These basics are the spice cabinet of the home bar.

**Angostura bitters:** Once a medicinal remedy, Angostura bitters grace many a timeless cocktail list and add a slight pungent flavor to mixed drinks.

**Baker's sugar:** This superfine sugar is an essential ingredient for my signature lollipop rim and easily mixes in handmade fruit purée recipes.

**Cerignola olives:** These exquisite Italian green olives are for when your friend who only drinks martinis ice cold and straight up comes to visit.

**Fresh lemons, limes, and oranges:** These fruits are often solicited as garnishes or muddled into the mix for strong fruit flavors.

**Fresh mint:** From mojitos to mint juleps, fresh mint is a refreshing addition to many cocktails.

**Kosher salt:** This course, flavorful salt makes an impressive salt rim for margaritas.

**Sugar cubes:** An essential ingredient to lightly sweeten cocktails.

## Simple Syrup

Used in many *Hip Sips* recipes, simple syrup is the binding agent for spirits, fresh citrus juices, and fruit purées and adds a subtle sweetness to cocktails.

**1 cup water**
**1 cup sugar**

In a small stainless-steel saucepan, combine the water and sugar. Stir with a wooden spoon over medium heat until the sugar has completely dissolved. Remove from the heat and let cool to room temperature. Pour the syrup into a glass bottle with a pour spout. Cap, refrigerate, and use as needed. Makes 14 ounces.

## Fresh Lemon-Lime Juice

Fresh lemon-lime juice is essential to many *Hip Sips* cocktails. Here are two recipes. One is for the Martha type who will risk carpal tunnel syndrome just to make sure that each ingredient is derived directly from its source. The second is for the on-the-go type who can successfully multitask a party for ten and a crisis of CNN proportions.

The key to both recipes is freshness. Remember that *Hip Sips* cocktails are based on fresh foods, not a liquid concentrate contrived in New Jersey by a scientist.

**10 lemons (about 10 ounces juice)**
**10 limes (about 10 ounces juice)**

Roll each fruit back and forth on the kitchen counter while pushing on the fruit to release the juices. Cut the fruit in half crosswise. Squeeze the juice into a medium bowl, using a handheld or stationary juicer. Combine the juices in a glass container and shake to thoroughly mix. Cover and store in the refrigerator for up to 48 hours. Makes 20 ounces.

### Easy-Way-Out Fresh Lemon-Lime Juice

**1 bottle (16 ounces) Santa Cruz 100% Lime Juice (see Sources)**
**1 bottle (16 ounces) Santa Cruz 100% Lemon Juice (see Sources)**

Combine the juices in a glass container. Shake vigorously to mix. Store in the refrigerator for up to 7 days. Makes 32 ounces.

# Fruit Purées

The foundation of most *Hip Sips* cocktails is fruit. The Sources section details where to purchase high-quality frozen purées, but if you've just returned from a Sunday filled with picking berries, try one of these recipes. Depending on the ripeness of the fruit, the amount of sugar in each recipe may need to be adjusted to taste.

### Berry Purée

**1 cup fresh blueberries, red currants, blackberries, or**
  **hulled strawberries**
**5 tablespoons water**
**2 tablespoons baker's sugar, plus more if needed**
**$^1/_4$ teaspoon fresh lemon juice, plus more if needed**

Combine the fruit, water, 2 tablespoons sugar, and $^1/_4$ teaspoon lemon juice in a blender and pulse until completely chopped. Purée until smooth. Taste the purée and add more sugar or lemon juice if needed. Strain through a sieve to remove the seeds. Use immediately, or freeze for up to 6 months. Makes 1$^1/_2$ cups.

### Melon Purée

**1$^1/_4$ cups cubed cantaloupe or honeydew melon**
**5 tablespoons water**
**1 tablespoon baker's sugar, plus more if needed**
**$^1/_4$ teaspoon fresh lemon juice, plus more if needed**

Combine the fruit, water, 1 tablespoon sugar, and $^1/_4$ teaspoon lemon juice in a blender and pulse until completely chopped. Purée until smooth. Taste the purée and add more sugar or lemon juice if needed. Use immediately, or freeze for up to 6 months. Makes 1 cup.

### Mandarin Purée

    **4 mandarin oranges (tangerines), peeled, segmented,**
      **and seeded if necessary**
    **1 tablespoon baker's sugar, plus more if needed**
    **1 teaspoon fresh lemon juice, plus more if needed**

Combine the fruit, 1 tablespoon sugar, and 1 teaspoon lemon juice in a blender and pulse the ingredients until completely chopped. Purée until smooth. Taste the purée and add more sugar or lemon juice if needed. Use immediately, or freeze for up to 6 months. Makes 1 cup.

### Mango or Guava Purée

    **2 mangos or guavas, peeled and pitted**
    **2 tablespoons baker's sugar, plus more if needed**
    **1 tablespoon water**
    **1 teaspoon fresh lemon juice, plus more if needed**

Combine the fruit, 2 tablespoons sugar, water, and 1 teaspoon lemon juice in a blender and pulse until completely chopped. Purée until smooth. Taste the purée and add more sugar or lemon juice if needed. Use immediately, or freeze for up to 6 months. Makes $1^1/_2$ cups.

### Fig Purée

    **2 cups fresh figs, stemmed and halved**
    **1 tablespoon baker's sugar, plus more if needed**
    **2 teaspoons water**
    **1 teaspoon fresh lemon juice, plus more if needed**

Combine the fruit, 1 tablespoon sugar, 2 teaspoons water, and 1 teaspoon lemon juice in a blender and pulse until completely chopped. Purée until smooth. Taste the purée and add more sugar or lemon juice if needed. Use immediately, or freeze for up to 6 months. Makes 1 cup.

### Passion Fruit Purée

- **2 passion fruits, peeled, seeded, and chopped**
- **2 tablespoons baker's sugar, plus more if needed**
- **1 tablespoon water**
- **2 teaspoons fresh lemon juice, plus more if needed**

Press the passion fruits through a sieve with the back of a wooden spoon. Combine the strained fruit, 2 tablespoons sugar, water, and 2 teaspoons lemon juice in a blender. Purée until smooth. Taste the purée and add more sugar or lemon juice if needed. Use immediately, or freeze for up to 6 months. Makes 1$^1$/$_2$ cups.

# Shake, Pop, Pour

On the age-old debate between shaken and stirred cocktails, I stand firmly on the side of shaken. Historically, conventional martini drinks are carefully stirred and never shaken. The reasoning behind this kid-gloves approach is a strongly held belief that shaking a martini bruises the spirit and causes the drink to lose its clarity.

*Hip Sips* are different. These cocktails require ingredients to be vigorously shaken. To thoroughly fuse fresh ingredients and create a cocktail with complexity and interest, you've got to shake the hell out of it.

My technique is short and sweet. These drinks are not shy, and neither should you be when trying your hand at a Ruby or a Mandarin Kiss. "Shake, pop, pour" will be your mantra.

Once you become proficient at the basics of making a *Hip Sips* cocktail, you'll find it easy to line up your tempered pint glasses packed with ice and make several cocktails at a time. It is not rocket science. The process is quick and easy, down and dirty.

1. Pack the pint glass with ice.

2. Add your ingredients.

3. Carefully place the stainless-steel cocktail shaker on top of the pint glass at about a 10-degree angle to the pint glass. (If you place the shaker directly on top of the pint glass, it will be very difficult to separate the two containers after you shake the cocktail.)

4. Quickly invert the shaker and the glass, dumping the ingredients into the shaker.

5. With the glasses still fitted together at an angle, raise the combo above your shoulder, securely holding the shaker on the bottom and the pint glass on the top with opposite hands. Arc the contents back and forth between the glass and shaker, shaking them for about 10 seconds.

6. Hold the shaker in front of you and, with the base of your palm, pop the shaker free of the pint glass with a quick hit. Do not hit the pint glass or you might cause it to break.

7. Use the shaker, as you would a saucepan lid, to strain the ice from the drink, pouring the cocktail into the cocktail glass.

Immediately after the drink is poured, you will notice a slight foam sitting pretty on top of the drink. This is the sign of a well-mixed drink and shake-pop-and-pour success. All the ingredients have been thoroughly fused. What you are about to taste is liquid bliss.

## Citrus Twists, Berry Pick, the Lollipop Rim, and the Salt Rim

Food-forward drinks deserve fashion-forward accessories. The essential *Hip Sips* wardrobe includes the up-to-date accoutrements of citrus twists, berry picks, and the signature lollipop rim, plus the beloved salt rim.

With *Hip Sips*, the anemic twist of the past is replaced with super-sized ribbons of lemon and lime zest. Berry picks replace stale white onion and green olive garnishes with a dainty skewer of berries placed artistically across the top of the glass. The lollipop rim is the diamond tiara of cocktails.

**Citrus twists:** Using a vegetable peeler, carve a 3- to 4-inch strip of zest, taking care not to include any of the bitter white pith. For a citrus grace note, gently pinch the twist and glide it across the lip of the glass. Before dropping the twist into the drink, squeeze it over the top.

**Berry pick:** Choose your favorite fresh in-season berry, be it raspberry, blackberry, cherry, or strawberry. Select 2 ripe berries of the same type. Carefully skewer each with the food pick, keeping the berries on the bottom half of the toothpick. Lay the berry pick across the edge of the glass to serve.

**Lollipop rim:** The lollipop rim is the signature garnish of many Hip Sips. Much more than a decorative side note, it's an important accent to the drink. The sugar lightly sweetens the tart flavors of ingredients such as passion fruit or green apple.

The lollipop rim works best on a 10-ounce martini glass. The oversized wide-mouthed glass is substantial enough to feature a generous 2-inch coating of sugar.

**1 cup baker's sugar**
**1 wedge lemon or orange**

Put the sugar in a moderately deep, wide-mouthed bowl. Make a deep slice down the center flesh of a lemon or orange wedge. Slightly squeeze the wedge to begin to release the juice. Place the slice on the rim of a 10-ounce martini glass and, holding the glass upside down, rotate the wedge around the glass to coat the rim with citrus juice. When you are finished, insert a quarter of the lip of the glass about 2 inches into the sugar. Quickly spin the stem to coat the entire rim with sugar. Lift the glass from the sugar, holding the cup upside down, and gently tap the bottom of the glass to remove any excess sugar.

**Salt rim:** Pour kosher salt 1-inch deep on a small plate. Make a slice down the center flesh of a lime wedge. Place the slice on the rim of the glass and rotate the wedge around the glass to coat the rim with lime juice. Dip the entire rim of the glass into the salt. Lift the glass from the salt and tap off any excess.

# Fruit Escapes

The following cocktails are a public service during a cold, dark winter. In a heroic attempt to fight off cabin fever, Fruit Escapes take you to Coco Cabana without having to leave the house. The next time you crave the sting of a sunburn, the scent of saltwater, and the sound of seagulls, close your eyes and slowly sip a Banana Drop or a Guava Cosmo.

Each cocktail in "Fruit Escapes" celebrates sunshine and the sometimes sweet, sometimes sour, always bold flavors of fresh fruit. So before you charge first-class tickets to a tropical island paradise or suggest Hawaiian-shirt Fridays at work, chant these words and start shakin': "On Vegas, on San Juan, on Cabo and Maui. On St. Bart's, on Rio, on Santa Monica and Hawaii. Now dash away gray skies. Dash away all."

# Splash

FIRE UP THE HIBACHI AND CANNONBALL INTO YOUR NEXT
POOL PARTY WITH THIS INSPIRED MARGARITA. FLAVORS
OF ALMOND AND MANDARIN ADD A SWEET, SMOKY FINISH
TO A WARM-WEATHER QUENCHER. TEST THE WATERS WITH
A SPICY CAESAR SALAD AND GRILLED PRAWNS, AND THE
SPLASH WILL HAVE YOU KICKING OFF YOUR FLIP-FLOPS
AND DIVING INTO SUMMER.

Serves 1

| | | |
|---|---|---|
| **Cocktail ice cubes for mixing and serving** | **1 ounce Fresh Lemon-Lime Juice (page 20)** | **1 lime slice for garnish** |
| **2 ounces Sauza Hornitos tequila** | **$1/2$ ounce Simple Syrup (page 20)** | |
| **$1/2$ ounce Amaretto liqueur** | **2 tablespoons Mandarin Purée (page 22)** | |

Fill a tempered pint glass with ice and add the tequila,
Amaretto, lemon-lime juice, simple syrup,
and mandarin purée. Cap the glass with a
stainless-steel cocktail shaker and shake
vigorously for 10 seconds. Pour the drink
and ice into a balloon wineglass. Garnish
with lime slice. Serve immediately, with a
straw.

# Bella

ONE OF THE MOST POPULAR COCKTAILS ON THE MENU AT
MINT, THIS ELEGANT COCKTAIL IS NAMED AFTER MY DOG,
BELLA. A TOUCH OF BLACKBERRY IN THE DRINK ADDS
JOIE DE VIVRE. FLOUNCY SKIRTS, HERMÈS SCARVES, AND
CROCODILE PUMPS PAIR EXCEPTIONALLY WELL WITH
THIS VIVACIOUS SIP.

*Serves 1*

| | | |
|---|---|---|
| Cocktail ice cubes for shaking | 1 ounce Fresh Lemon-Lime Juice (page 20) | **GARNISH**<br>Lollipop Rim (page 25) |
| 2 ounces Monopolowa vodka | 1 ounce Simple Syrup (page 20) | 1 blackberry or marionberry Berry Pick (page 25) for garnish |
| ¼ ounce Harlequin orange liqueur | 2 tablespoons Blackberry Purée (page 21) | |

Fill a tempered pint glass with ice and add the vodka,
liqueur, lemon-lime juice, simple syrup,
and blackberry purée. Cap the glass with a
stainless-steel cocktail shaker and shake
vigorously for 10 seconds. Strain the drink
into a 10-ounce martini glass garnished
with a lollipop rim and the berry pick. Serve
immediately.

# TriBeCa

THIS TRIBUTE TO THE MANHATTAN COMBINES THE SPICE AND VANILLA FLAVORS OF BOURBON WITH THE HONEY-SWEET TEXTURE AND FLAVOR OF A RIPE GREEN MELON. IT'S ECLECTIC AND CHARMING, MUCH LIKE ITS NAMESAKE NEW YORK CITY NEIGHBORHOOD. THIS DRINK PAIRS WELL AS A STARTER WITH TOASTED PUMPKIN SEEDS OR, FOR DINNER, A FLATIRON STEAK. FOR A MORE PRONOUNCED MELON FLAVOR, SUBSTITUTE CANTALOUPE PURÉE FOR THE HONEYDEW MELON PURÉE.

*Serves 1*

Cocktail ice cubes for chilling and shaking

2 1/2 ounces Jim Beam bourbon

1/2 ounce Fresh Lemon-Lime Juice (page 20)

1/2 ounce Simple Syrup (page 20)

2 tablespoons honeydew Melon Purée (page 21)

Dash of Angostura bitters

1 lemon slice for garnish

Fill a 5-ounce martini glass with ice and set aside to chill. Fill a tempered pint glass with ice and add the bourbon, lemon-lime juice, simple syrup, melon purée, and bitters. Cap the pint glass with a stainless-steel cocktail shaker and shake vigorously for 10 seconds. Empty the ice from the martini glass. Strain the mixed drink into the chilled glass. Garnish with the lemon slice and serve immediately.

# 816

I NAMED THIS DRINK AFTER MY RESTAURANT'S STREET
ADDRESS, 816 NORTH RUSSELL STREET. ONE OF THE MOST
POPULAR COCKTAILS ON THE MENU THERE, THIS SOPHIS-
TICATED INTERPRETATION OF THE ALMIGHTY LEMON DROP
WILL SHOCK YOUR TASTE BUDS INTO SUBMISSION.
SEDUCTIVE CITRUS SPIRITS OF GREY GOOSE LE CITRON
AND HARLEQUIN WRAP THEMSELVES AROUND THE PURÉE
LIKE A SAUCY FLIRT. SO IF YOUR EVENING OUT INCLUDES
NEON LIGHTS, START IT OFF WITH AN 816.

*Serves 1*

| | | |
|---|---|---|
| Cocktail ice cubes for shaking | 1 ounce Fresh Lemon-Lime Juice (page 20) | Lollipop Rim (page 25) for garnish |
| 2 1/2 ounces Grey Goose Le Citron vodka | 1 ounce Simple Syrup (page 20) | |
| 1/4 ounce Harlequin orange liqueur | 2 tablespoons Passion Fruit Purée (page 23) | |

Fill a tempered pint glass with ice and add the vodka,
liqueur, lemon-lime juice, simple syrup,
and passion fruit purée. Cap the glass with
a stainless-steel cocktail shaker and shake
vigorously for 10 seconds. Strain into a
10-ounce martini glass garnished with a
lollipop rim. Serve immediately.

# Mandarin Kiss

THIS DRINK IS A TOAST TO ODD COUPLES. THE SMOKE AND SPICE OF BOURBON MATCHES MAGICALLY WITH THE TANGY SWEETNESS OF MANDARIN. WHEN PAIRED WITH A LAMB BURGER, THIS DRINK LETS YOU KNOW THAT EVEN TOUGH GUYS LIKE THEIR COCKTAILS SEALED WITH A KISS.

Serves 1

Cocktail ice cubes for shaking and serving

2 ounces Maker's Mark bourbon

2 tablespoons Mandarin Purée (page 22)

Splash of soda water

1 orange slice for garnish

Fill a tempered pint glass with ice and add the bourbon and mandarin purée. Cap the glass with a stainless-steel cocktail shaker and shake vigorously for 10 seconds. Pour the drink and ice into a bucket glass, leaving about 1 inch of space at the top of the glass. Top off the drink with the soda water. Garnish with the orange slice. Serve immediately.

# Banana Drop

YOUR VINYL-WEAVE LOUNGE CHAIR HASN'T SEEN ANY
ACTION SINCE LABOR DAY WEEKEND, AND YOUR
SUNSCREEN HAS COAGULATED IN THE BOTTLE. BANANA
DROP SEASON STARTS THE MOMENT YOU REALIZE THAT
SPIDERS ARE BUILDING INTRICATE HOUSING DEVELOP-
MENTS IN YOUR GAS GRILL, AND YOU STILL HAVE MONTHS
TO GO UNTIL SPRING BREAK. THE NEXT TIME THE WINTER
DOLDRUMS HAVE YOU FEELING LIKE YOU'RE TRAPPED
INDOORS, TRY THIS SWEET, SOULFUL TROPICAL REMEDY
AND REMEMBER THAT SUNSHINE IS ONLY A TASTE AWAY.

Serves 1

Cocktail ice cubes
for shaking

2 ounces Cruzan
banana rum

1/4 ounce Harlequin
orange liqueur

1 ounce Fresh Lemon-
Lime Juice (page 20)

1 ounce Simple Syrup
(page 20)

Lollipop Rim (page 25)
for garnish

Fill a tempered pint glass with ice and add the rum,
liqueur, lemon-lime juice, and simple
syrup. Cap the glass with a stainless-steel
cocktail shaker and shake vigorously for
10 seconds. Strain into a 10-ounce martini
glass garnished with a lollipop rim. Serve
immediately.

# Passion Fruit Twirl

PASSION FRUIT SPIKES THIS SUNDAY-MORNING WAKE-UP
CALL WITH VIBRANT FLAVORS. THIS BUBBLY COCKTAIL
ADDS PURE LUXURY AND LOTS OF POP TO A LAZY BRUNCH
AND IS AN EXTROVERTED COMPANION TO A SPANISH
OMELET OR A FRITTATA.

*Serves 1*

**Cocktail ice cubes for shaking and serving**

**1¹/₂ ounces vodka**

**1 ounce Fresh Lemon-Lime Juice (page 20)**

**1 ounce Simple Syrup (page 20)**

**2 tablespoons Passion Fruit Purée (page 23)**

**Splash of cranberry juice**

**1 ounce chilled Champagne**

**1 orange slice for garnish**

Fill a tempered pint glass with ice and add the vodka, lemon-lime juice, simple syrup, passion fruit purée, and cranberry juice. Cap the glass with a stainless-steel cocktail shaker and shake vigorously for 10 seconds. Pour the drink and ice into a Collins glass, leaving about 1 inch of space at the top of the glass. Top off the drink with the Champagne. Garnish with the orange slice and serve immediately.

# Freestyle

FLAVORS OF CINNAMON AND MANDARIN ADD JUST
ENOUGH HEAT, SPICE, AND CITRUS TO HINT AT THE END OF
FALL AND GRACIOUSLY USHER YOU INTO WINTER. SERVE
WITH A PAN-SEARED PORK CHOP AND MOLE SAUCE.

*Serves 1*

Cocktail ice cubes for shaking

2 ounces Cruzan mango rum

¼ ounce Harlequin orange liqueur

1 ounce Fresh Lemon-Lime Juice (page 20)

1 ounce Simple Syrup (page 20)

2 tablespoons Mango Purée (page 22)

1 tablespoon Mandarin Purée (page 22)

3 dashes ground cinnamon, plus dash for garnish

Lollipop Rim (page 25) for garnish

Fill a tempered pint glass with ice and add the rum, liqueur, lemon-lime juice, simple syrup, mango purée, and mandarin purée. Top with the 3 dashes of cinnamon. Cap the glass with a stainless-steel cocktail shaker and shake vigorously for 10 seconds. Strain into a 10-ounce martini glass garnished with a lollipop rim. Add another dash of cinnamon and serve immediately.

# Pineapple Drop

THE PINEAPPLE DROP CAN MINGLE SKILLFULLY AT
ANY OCCASION, HIGHBROW OR LOWBROW, MAKING
THE ROUNDS AT A NANTUCKET SOIRÉE OR A BACKYARD
BIRTHDAY PARTY. THE DRINK'S ANIMATED PERSONALITY
COMES THROUGH IN EACH SIP AND WILL ACCOMPANY
A PULLED-PORK SANDWICH AND SLAW OR A FILET
WRAPPED IN BACON WITH EQUAL GRACE.

Serves 1

Cocktail ice cubes for shaking

2 ounces Cruzan pineapple rum

¼ ounce Harlequin orange liqueur

1 ounce Fresh Lemon-Lime Juice (page 20)

1 ounce Simple Syrup (page 20)

1 ounce pineapple juice

Lollipop Rim (page 25) for garnish

Fill a tempered pint glass with ice and add the rum, liqueur, lemon-lime juice, simple syrup, and pineapple juice. Cap the glass with a stainless-steel cocktail shaker and shake vigorously for 10 seconds. Strain the mixed drink into a 10-ounce martini glass garnished with a lollipop rim. Serve immediately.

# Charlie

WITH SLIGHTLY LESS CITRUS THAN A TRADITIONAL MARGARITA, THE CHARLIE MAKES UP FOR IT WITH THE GRACEFULLY TART SWEETNESS OF THE RASPBERRY PURÉE, WHICH PAIRS EXCEPTIONALLY WELL WITH CHOCOLATE FONDUE OR A RICH FLAN.

*Serves 1*

**Cocktail ice cubes for shaking and serving**

**2 ounces gold tequila**

**¼ ounce Harlequin orange liqueur**

**1 ounce Fresh Lemon-Lime Juice (page 20)**

**1 ounce Simple Syrup (page 20)**

**2 tablespoons Raspberry Purée (page 21)**

**2 lime slices for garnish**

Fill a tempered pint glass with ice and add the tequila, liqueur, lemon-lime juice, simple syrup, and raspberry purée. Cap the glass with a stainless-steel cocktail shaker and shake vigorously for 10 seconds. Pour both drink and ice into a tumbler or balloon wineglass. Garnish with the lime slices and serve immediately.

# Velvet

THE DENSELY FRAGRANT VELVET ENTICES THE PALATE WITH THE FLORAL IMPRESSIONS OF BLACKBERRY AND VANILLA SPICE. FOR A PERFECT LATE-AFTERNOON INDULGENCE, PAIR THE VELVET WITH BUTTERY SHORT-BREAD COOKIES.

*Serves* 1

Cocktail ice cubes for shaking and serving

2 ounces vodka

1 ounce Fresh Lemon-Lime Juice (page 20)

³/₄ ounce Monin vanilla syrup (see Sources)

2 tablespoons Blackberry Purée (page 21)

Splash of cranberry juice

**GARNISH**

1 orange slice

1 blackberry Berry Pick (page 25)

Fill a tempered pint glass with ice and add the vodka, lemon-lime juice, vanilla syrup, blackberry purée, and cranberry juice. Cap the glass with a stainless-steel cocktail shaker and shake vigorously for 10 seconds. Pour the drink and ice into a Collins glass. Garnish the drink with the orange slice and berry pick. Serve immediately.

# Guava Cosmo

ONE PART *SEX IN THE CITY* AND ONE PART *FANTASY ISLAND*, THIS CARIBBEAN COSMOPOLITAN WILL HAVE YOU SLIPPING ON YOUR MANOLOS AND CRYING "THE PLANE, THE PLANE!" AT THE SAME TIME. INDULGENCE SAILS THROUGH EACH SIP WITH SMOOTHIELIKE SENSATIONS. SMILES, EVERYONE, SMILES.

 *Serves 1*

**Cocktail ice cubes for shaking**

**2 1/2 ounces vodka**

**1/4 ounce Harlequin orange liqueur**

**1 ounce Fresh Lemon-Lime Juice (page 20)**

**1 ounce Simple Syrup (page 20)**

**2 tablespoons Guava Purée (page 22)**

**Splash of cranberry juice**

**1 lime wedge for garnish**

Fill a tempered pint glass with ice and add the vodka, liqueur, lemon-lime juice, simple syrup, guava purée, and cranberry juice. Cap the glass with a stainless-steel cocktail shaker and shake vigorously for 10 seconds. Strain into a 10-ounce martini glass and garnish with a lime wedge. Serve immediately.

# Mirrorball

RING IN THE NEW YEAR WITH THIS SPUNKY COMBINATION
OF WATERMELON-INFUSED VODKA AND CHAMPAGNE. EACH
SIP SPARKLES AND WILL INCITE YOUR PARTY GUESTS TO A
FEVERED PITCH, JUST IN TIME FOR THE BALL TO DROP.

*Serves 1*

Cocktail ice cubes for shaking

2 ounces Watermelon-Infused Vodka (recipe follows)

1/4 ounce Harlequin orange liqueur

1 ounce Fresh Lemon-Lime Juice (page 20)

1 ounce Simple Syrup (page 20)

Splash of cranberry juice

1 ounce Champagne

**FOR THE WATERMELON-INFUSED VODKA**

One 10-pound watermelon, peeled, seeded, and cut into 2-inch chunks (10 cups)

1 bottle (1 liter) Monopolowa vodka

*Fill a tempered pint glass with ice and add the vodka, liqueur,* lemon-lime juice, simple syrup, and cranberry juice. Cap the glass with a stainless-steel cocktail shaker and shake vigorously for 10 seconds. Strain the drink into a 10-ounce martini glass. Top off with the Champagne. Serve immediately.

*Watermelon-Infused Vodka* Put the watermelon in a wide-mouthed glass jar with a lid. (2-gallon storage jars work well.) Add the vodka and seal the container. (Reserve the vodka bottle for refilling.) Store in a cool, dark place for 3 days. Using a slotted spoon, transfer the watermelon to a fine-meshed sieve. Press on the solids with the back of a large spoon to push the pulp through the sieve. Return the purée to the vodka in the container. Place a funnel in the reserved vodka bottle and pour the infused vodka back into the bottle and seal the top. Shake the vodka to mix any settled watermelon before you add it to a drink. Store in the refrigerator for up to 6 months. *Makes 1 liter*

# Brave New World:

## Where the Kitchen and the Bar Collide

When your cocktail ingredients look more like a grocery list than a run to the liquor store, you've entered a *brave new world* where the kitchen and the bar collide. Rum is finally liberated from Coke and gains cult status in an *Avocado Daiquiri*. Ruby port is introduced to figs to celebrate the turning of the leaves, and rhubarb meets gin just in time for the tulips to bloom.

Concocting food-forward cocktails is for the bold soul who loves the thrill of invention and the goal of surprising the most guarded palates. Whether seeking out the season's ripe fruits or discovering a novel way to enjoy a locally distilled spirit, twenty-first-century mixologists are eager to wake up a tired cocktail list and be the hit of the next housewarming party. These drinks are an invitation to take a closer look at your favorite fruits and vegetables and to meet your local spirit craftspeople. See what happens when you *shake things up*.

# Avocado Daiquiri

AT LEAST ONE DAIQUIRI HAS MADE ITS WAY OUT OF THE
TIKI BARS AND ONTO SOPHISTICATED DINNER MENUS.
TRY THIS DELIGHTFUL DRINK WITH A BURGER OR SPICY
CEVICHE. THE KEY TO MAKING THIS LIGHTLY SWEET, SILKY
SMOOTH DAIQUIRI IS A PERFECTLY RIPE AVOCADO. AN
UNDERRIPE ONE LACKS THE DELICATE FLAVOR ESSENTIAL
TO THE DRINK, AND AN OVERRIPE ONE MAY LEAVE THE
DAIQUIRI A DISCOLORED TAN. THE AVOCADO SHOULD BE
FIRM BUT SLIGHTLY SOFT TO THE TOUCH. DISCARD ANY
BROWN SPOTS BEFORE ADDING THE AVOCADO.

*Serves 1*

2 ounces silver rum

2 ounces gold rum

1/4 medium-ripe
avocado, peeled and
pitted

1/2 ounce half-and-half

1/4 ounce Fresh Lemon-
Lime Juice (page 20)

2 ounces Simple Syrup
(page 20)

1 1/2 cups cocktail ice
cubes

Pomegranate concen-
trate (see Sources)
for garnish

In a blender, combine the rums, avocado, half-and-half,
lemon-lime juice, and simple syrup. Add the
ice and blend for 20 to 30 seconds or until the
mixture is silky smooth with no trace of ice.
The consistency of the drink should be similar
to heavy cream. Pour into a balloon wineglass
and lightly zigzag pomegranate concentrate
over the top. Place a small drink straw or
toothpick at the top of the zigzag pattern and
pull through the center to make a series of
pomegranate hearts. Serve immediately.

# "Ad Lib"

DURING A VODKA COCKTAIL COMPETITION, I SPONTANEOUSLY CREATED THE "AD LIB" AND WON FIRST PRIZE. THE DRINK HAS SINCE BECOME A REFRESHING PATIO-SEASON STAPLE AT MY RESTAURANT MINT. THE CILANTRO IS FIRST MUDDLED TO RELEASE ITS SPICY BITE, THEN SHAKEN WITH VODKA, SIMPLE SYRUP, AND LEMON-LIME JUICE. A FRESH ALTERNATIVE TO MARGARITAS, THE "AD LIB" IS A GREAT REMINDER THAT YOUR NEXT FAVORITE COCKTAIL MAY BE A GLORIOUS ACCIDENT.

*Serves 1*

| | |
|---|---|
| **Cocktail ice cubes for muddling and shaking** | **1 ounce Fresh Lemon-Lime Juice (page 20)** |
| **5 to 7 fresh cilantro leaves** | **1 ounce Simple Syrup (page 20)** |
| **2½ ounces Crater Lake vodka** | **Lollipop Rim (page 25) for garnish** |

*Fill a tempered pint glass with ice and add the cilantro.* Muddle (see page 15) until the ice is slushy and the cilantro is evenly distributed throughout the ice. Add ice to fill the glass. Add the vodka, lemon-lime juice, and simple syrup. Cap the glass with a stainless-steel cocktail shaker and shake vigorously for 10 seconds. Strain into a 10-ounce martini glass garnished with a lollipop rim. Serve immediately.

# Sweet Love

Serves 1

NO COCKTAIL LIST IS COMPLETE WITHOUT AT LEAST ONE COFFEE DRINK, ESPECIALLY IN THE PACIFIC NORTHWEST, HOME OF INDEPENDENT COFFEE SHOPS AND MICRO-ROASTERS. SWEET LOVE IS AN IRRESISTIBLE ALTERNATIVE TO THE REVERED FLAMING SPANISH COFFEE, AND YOU WON'T HAVE TO WORRY ABOUT BURNING DOWN THE HOUSE. THE RICH FLAVORS OF SWEET BANANA, TOASTED CHOCOLATE, AND VANILLA CREAM UNFOLD IN EACH SEDUCTIVE GULP. ONE MOUTHFUL OF THIS COCKTAIL WILL HAVE YOU SKIPPING DESSERT.

1 ounce Kahlúa liqueur

1 ounce Cruzan banana rum

3 ounces strong hot coffee

**GARNISH**

2 heaping tablespoons Vanilla Whipped Cream (recipe follows)

Mexican chocolate shavings

**FOR THE VANILLA WHIPPED CREAM**

1 cup heavy (whipping) cream

1/4 ounce Monin vanilla syrup

Pour the Kahlúa and rum into a 12-ounce heat-resistant wineglass. Add the coffee, leaving a 1-inch space at the top of the glass. Add the whipped cream and a generous amount of chocolate shavings. Lay 2 long drinking straws across the top of the drink. Hold the hot drink by the stem of the glass when serving.

## Vanilla Whipped Cream

In a chilled stainless-steel bowl, beat the cream with an electric mixer on high speed. As the cream begins to thicken, gradually add the vanilla syrup and beat until soft peaks form.

*Makes 2 cups*

# Absolut Mission

THIS SWEATER-WEATHER COCKTAIL WAS INSPIRED BY THE
EARTHY FIG AND CAPTURES MEMORIES OF RAKING
LEAVES AND STOKING FIRES. THE WARM SPICE OF VANILLA
COMBINED WITH THE SWEETNESS OF RUBY PORT AND
FIGS IMBUES THIS DRINK WITH THE FLAVORS OF FALL.
PAIR WITH DRY AGED CHEESES FOR YOUR NEXT KNITTING
CIRCLE AND PURL AWAY.

Serves 1

**Cocktail ice cubes for chilling and shaking**

**2 ounces Absolut Vanilla vodka**

**¹/₂ ounce ruby port**

**2 tablespoons Fig Purée (page 22)**

**¹/₂ ounce Fresh Lemon-Lime Juice (page 20)**

**¹/₂ ounce Simple Syrup (page 20)**

**1 edible flower or sliced fig for garnish**

Fill a 5-ounce martini glass with ice and set aside to
chill. Fill a tempered pint glass with ice and
add the vodka, port, fig purée, lemon-lime
juice, and simple syrup. Cap the glass with
a stainless-steel shaker and shake vigorously for 10 seconds. Empty the ice from
the martini glass. Strain the drink into the
chilled glass and garnish with a flower or
sliced fig. Serve immediately.

# Ruby

THE RUBY JUST MIGHT BE THE BEST COMBINATION OF CHILLED VODKA AND BEETS TO HIT THE STREETS SINCE PERESTROIKA. EARTHY UNDERTONES OF HANDMADE BEET-INFUSED VODKA GROUND THIS DIRTY MARTINI ALTERNATIVE. SERVE STRAIGHT UP WITH A MIXED GREEN SALAD, OR CROSTINI AND AGED CHEESES.

*Serves 1*

Cocktail ice cubes for chilling and shaking

3 ounces Beet-Infused Vodka (recipe page 56)

1/2 ounce Fresh Lemon-Lime Juice (page 20)

1/2 ounce Simple Syrup (page 20)

**FOR THE BEET-INFUSED VODKA**

3 red beets (1 1/2 pounds), trimmed, peeled, and cut into quarters

1 bottle (1 liter) Monopolowa vodka

Fill a 5-ounce martini glass with ice and set aside to chill. Fill a tempered pint glass with ice and add the vodka, lemon-lime juice, and simple syrup. Cap the glass with a stainless-steel cocktail shaker and shake vigorously for 10 seconds. Empty the ice from the martini glass. Strain the drink into the chilled glass and serve immediately.

*cont'd*

*Beet-Infused Vodka* Put the beets in a wide-mouthed glass jar with a lid, such as a 2-gallon storage jar. Add the vodka and seal the container. (Reserve the vodka bottle for refilling.) The mixture will immediately turn a bright ruby color. Store in a cool, dark place for 3 days, stirring each day. The infused vodka will be a deep purple color with a strong, earthy beet taste. Using a slotted spoon, remove and discard the beets. Place a funnel in the reserved vodka bottle and pour the infused vodka into the bottle. Cap and store in the refrigerator for up to 6 months.

*Makes 1 liter*

# Hazel

OREGON'S STATE NUT STARS IN THIS AFTER-DINNER
DELIGHT. BENDISTILLERY'S CRATER LAKE HAZELNUT
ESPRESSO VODKA BLENDS THE HIGH-OCTANE IMPACT OF
ESPRESSO WITH NOTES OF TOASTED HAZELNUT. VANILLA
RUM DIFFUSES THE LIQUEUR, ADDING SUGAR AND SPICE TO
THE DRINK. TRY PAIRING THE HAZEL WITH DARK CHOCOLATE
TRUFFLES IF YOU WANT YOUR DATE TO STAY THE NIGHT.

*Serves 1*

**Cocktail ice cubes for chilling and shaking**

**2 ounces Cruzan vanilla rum**

**1 ounce Crater Lake hazelnut espresso vodka (see Sources)**

**1 espresso bean for garnish**

Fill a 5-ounce martini glass with ice and set aside to chill. Fill a tempered pint glass with ice and add the rum and vodka. Cap the pint glass with a stainless-steel cocktail shaker and shake vigorously for 10 seconds. Empty the ice from the martini glass. Strain the drink into the chilled glass, add the espresso bean, and serve immediately.

# Heaven

THIS WORLD TRAVELER DOTES ON SPECIALTY LIQUEURS
FROM ITALY, JAMAICA, AND IRELAND AND IS A FESTIVE
COMPANION TO LATE-NIGHT CHATS. THE SWEET VANILLA
AND ORANGE FLAVORS OF TUACA, THE CREAMY, NUTTY
TASTES OF SAINT BRENDAN'S, AND THE COFFEE DELIGHT
OF TIA MARIA WILL HAVE YOU UP ALL NIGHT SHARING
CONFIDENCES AND SPINNING YARNS.

*Serves 1*

$^1/_2$ ounce Tuaca brandy

1 ounce Tia Maria
liqueur

1 ounce Saint Brendan's
Irish Cream liqueur

3 ounces strong hot
coffee

2 heaping tablespoons
Vanilla Whipped Cream
(see page 53)

In an 8-ounce heat-resistant wineglass, combine the
3 liqueurs. Top with the coffee, leaving a
1-inch space at the top of the glass. Add
the whipped cream. Serve with a straw, and
hold the hot glass by the stem.

# Fresh

PUCKER UP TO THIS REFRESHING INTERPRETATION OF THE APPLE MARTINI. THE PUNCH OF SOUR APPLE IS QUICKLY SOOTHED WITH COOL FLAVORS OF MUDDLED MINT. THE LOLLIPOP RIM IS ESSENTIAL IN ITS SUPPORTING ROLE OF TAMING THE TART FLAVORS. THIS SWEET-AND-SOUR COMBO IS ESPECIALLY APPROPRIATE WITH A RICH VANILLA ICE CREAM.

*Serves* 1

Cocktail ice cubes for muddling and shaking

5 to 7 fresh mint leaves

2 ounces Smirnoff apple vodka (not apple schnapps)

1 ounce Fresh Lemon-Lime Juice (page 20)

1 ounce Simple Syrup (page 20)

Lollipop Rim (page 25) for garnish

Fill a tempered pint glass one-fourth full with ice and add the mint. Muddle (see page 15) until the ice and mint mixture is slushy and the mint is evenly distributed throughout. Add ice to fill the glass. Add the vodka, lemon-lime juice, and simple syrup. Cap the glass with a stainless-steel cocktail shaker and shake vigorously for 10 seconds. Strain into a 10-ounce martini glass garnished with a lollipop rim. Serve immediately.

# Violet

THIS DENSE BLUEBERRY-FILLED DRINK STANDS ALONE AS
AN ALTERNATIVE DESSERT COURSE OR A MEMORABLE
APRÈS-THEATER TREAT. ONE RICH, SMOOTH VIOLET IS
QUITE ENOUGH, MATCHING TART BLUEBERRIES WITH
ORANGE AND CREAM.

*Serves 1*

**Cocktail ice cubes
for shaking**

**2 ounces Cruzan
orange rum**

**2 tablespoons
Blueberry Purée
(page 21)**

**1 ounce half-and-half**

**1 orange slice for
garnish**

Fill a tempered pint glass with ice and add the rum,
blueberry purée, and half-and-half. Cap
the glass with a stainless-steel cocktail
shaker and shake vigorously for 10 seconds.
Strain the drink into a 5-ounce martini
glass. Garnish with an orange slice and
serve immediately.

# Ivo

OPEN-TOE SHOE SEASON WILL NEVER BE THE SAME. PAIR
THIS DISTANT COUSIN OF THE CLASSIC LEMON DROP WITH
MANGO SALSA AND CHIPS OR A SPICY SHRIMP COCKTAIL
AND WATCH YOUR PATIO PARTY TAKE OFF.

*Serves 1*

| | | |
|---|---|---|
| Cocktail ice cubes for shaking | 1 ounce Simple Syrup (page 20) | **GARNISH** Lollipop Rim (page 25) |
| 2 ounces Cruzan vanilla rum | ¼ ounce Harlequin orange liqueur | 1 lemon slice |
| 1 ounce Fresh Lemon-Lime Juice (page 20) | | |

Fill a tempered pint glass with ice and add the rum, lemon-lime juice, simple syrup, and liqueur. Cap the glass with a stainless-steel shaker and shake vigorously for 10 seconds. Strain into a 10-ounce martini glass garnished with a lollipop rim. Garnish with the lemon slice and serve immediately.

# Spanish Armada

DON'T LET THE COFFEE AND CREAM COMBO FOOL YOU INTO CHOOSING THIS COCKTAIL FOR A NIGHTCAP. THE SPANISH ARMADA IS THE SPARK PLUG FOR A LIVELY BEFORE-DINNER CONVERSATION. PATRÓN XO CAFÉ IS AN EXCEPTIONAL COFFEE TEQUILA WITH STRONG BURNT-NUT FLAVORS. THE NUTMEG GARNISH IS ESSENTIAL TO BRINGING FORWARD NOTES OF THE TEQUILA.

Serves 1

**Cocktail ice cubes for shaking**

**2 ounces Patrón XO Café tequila**

**1 ounce half-and-half**

**Freshly grated nutmeg for garnish**

Fill a tempered pint glass with ice and add the tequila and the half-and-half. Cap the glass with a stainless-steel cocktail shaker and shake vigorously for 10 seconds. Strain into a 5-ounce martini glass. Garnish with nutmeg and serve immediately.

# Love on the Rocks

NAMED FOR THE FRENCH LIQUEUR PARFAIT AMOUR, THIS
SOFT-SPOKEN DRINK'S FLORAL BOUQUETS OF ORANGE
BLOSSOMS AND VANILLA FLATTER EACH OTHER.

*Serves* 1

**Cocktail ice cubes
for shaking and
serving**

**1 ounce Absolut
vanilla vodka**

**1/2 ounce Parfait
Amour liqueur**

**1/2 ounce cranberry
juice**

**1/2 ounce pineapple
juice**

Fill a tempered pint glass with ice and add the vodka,
liqueur, and juices. Cap the glass with a
stainless-steel cocktail shaker and shake
vigorously for 10 seconds. Pour the drink
and ice into a bucket glass. Serve with a
straw.

# Rhubarb Cooler

REVEL IN THE RITES OF SPRING WITH THIS INVIGORATING SPIN ON THE CLASSIC COLLINS. THIS COCKTAIL IS THE PERFECT TOAST TO HONOR THE FARMERS' MARKETS OF SPRING.

*Serves 1*

Cocktail ice cubes for chilling and shaking

1½ ounces gin

½ ounce Fresh Lemon-Lime Juice (page 20)

1 ounce Rhubarb Syrup (recipe follows)

Splash of soda water

1 lime wedge for garnish

**FOR THE RHUBARB SYRUP**

6 stalks rhubarb, cut into 1-inch pieces

2 cups baker's sugar

2 cups water

*Fill a Collins glass with ice and set aside.*

Fill a tempered pint glass with ice and add the gin, lemon-lime juice, and rhubarb syrup. Cap the glass with a stainless-steel cocktail shaker and shake vigorously for 10 seconds. Pour the drink with ice into the Collins glass. Garnish with the lime wedge and serve immediately.

## Rhubarb Syrup

In a medium stainless-steel saucepan, combine all the ingredients and bring to a boil over high heat. Reduce heat to a simmer and cook for 15 minutes, or until the rhubarb is very tender and the liquid coats the back of a spoon. Remove from heat and let cool to room temperature. Strain through a fine-meshed sieve into a glass container. Use now, or cover and refrigerate for up to 1 month.

Makes 3 cups

# Lucy's Twists

The cocktail's humble beginnings were often more of an attempt to dilute liquor with soda, water, or fruit juices than a culinary science or fashion. Since the liquor may have come from an illegal still, bartenders of the past didn't always take into consideration how to match the intricacies of *different spirits* with distinctive flavor components.

*Lucy's Twists* are insightful examples of what happens when hundred-year-old cocktail recipes get a second chance. A hint of hot sauce in a classic whiskey sour or notes of herbal Chartreuse liqueur and lime in an ice-cold vodka martini add a completely different character to the cocktail and take your palate down an unexpected road.

The result will be a pleasant surprise. These twists on classics are playgrounds of tempo and tone. Each tap-dancing note layers a new rhythm of flavor on your tongue.

# Hot and Sour

SOME LIKE IT HOT, AND THAT IS EXACTLY WHAT THIS
HANDCRAFTED WHISKEY SOUR DELIVERS. SWEET-AND-
SOUR GULPS ARE THE OPENING ACT. THE SURPRISE
ENDING KICKS IN JUST WHEN YOU THINK THE FINISH
IS COMPLETE.

| | | |
|---|---|---|
| 1 sugar cube | Cocktail ice cubes for muddling and shaking | 1 ounce Simple Syrup (page 20) |
| 5 dashes Angostura bitters | 3 ounces Maker's Mark bourbon | Dash of Tabasco sauce |
| 1/4 lemon | 1 ounce Fresh Lemon-Lime Juice (page 20) | **GARNISH** |
| 2 maraschino cherries, stemmed | | Lollipop Rim (page 25) |
| | | 2 maraschino cherries |

Put the sugar cube in a tempered pint glass and coat
the cube thoroughly with the bitters. Add
the lemon wedge, cherries, and 1/2 cup ice
cubes. Muddle (see page 15) until the ice is
red and slushy. Fill the glass with ice. Add
the bourbon, lemon-lime juice, simple syrup,
and Tabasco. Cap the glass with a stainless-
steel cocktail shaker and shake vigorously for
10 seconds. Strain into a 10-ounce martini
glass garnished with a lollipop rim. Garnish
with the cherries and serve immediately.

# Anniversario Manhattan

PAMPERO ANNIVERSARIO, A VENEZUELAN RUM AGED IN FRENCH OAK, IS AN EXQUISITE SELECTION FOR A WORLDLY MANHATTAN. SIMILAR TO A FINE WINE, THIS RUM OPENS AND EVOLVES AS IT IS EXPOSED TO AIR INSIDE THE COCKTAIL GLASS.

*Serves 1*

**Cocktail ice cubes for chilling and shaking**

**2 1/2 ounces Pampero Anniversario rum**

**1/4 ounce sweet vermouth**

**3 dashes Angostura bitters**

**1 maraschino cherry for garnish**

Fill a 5-ounce martini glass with ice and set aside to chill. Fill a tempered pint glass with ice and add the rum, vermouth, and bitters. Cap the glass with a stainless-steel cocktail shaker and shake vigorously for 10 seconds. Empty the ice from the martini glass. Strain the drink into the chilled glass. Garnish with the cherry and serve immediately.

# O

THE O IS THE CARMEN MIRANDA OF CITRUS
COCKTAILS, A HIP-SHAKING INVITATION TO
CHA-CHA THE NIGHT AWAY.

*Serves 1*

Cocktail ice cubes for
shaking and serving

6 fresh mint leaves

2 ounces Cruzan
orange rum

1 ounce Fresh Lemon-
Lime Juice (page 20)

1 ounce Simple Syrup
(page 20)

Splash of soda water

1 orange slice for
garnish

Fill a tempered pint glass one-fourth full with ice and add the mint leaves. Fill the glass with ice. Add the rum, lemon-lime juice, and simple syrup. Cap the glass with a stainless-steel cocktail shaker and shake vigorously for 10 seconds. Pour the drink and ice into a Collins glass. Top off with the soda water. Garnish with the orange slice and serve.

# Vermont

THE TOAST AND NUT NUANCES OF THE VERMONT WILL OPEN YOUR EYES TO A WORLD WHERE MAPLE SYRUP TAKES ON A LIFE OUTSIDE OF THE BREAKFAST TABLE. THE COCKTAIL IS ONLY AS GOOD AS THE MAPLE SYRUP IT IS MADE WITH, SO GRAB THE FINEST JUG OF GRADE A THAT YOU CAN FIND. YOUR PANCAKES WILL THANK YOU FOR IT, TOO.

*Serves 1*

**Cocktail ice cubes for chilling and shaking**

**3 ounces Grey Goose vodka**

**¼ ounce Grade A Vermont maple syrup**

**1 unsalted Spanish almond for garnish**

*Fill a 5-ounce martini glass with ice and set aside to* chill. Fill a tempered pint glass with ice and add the vodka and maple syrup. Cap the glass with a stainless-steel cocktail shaker and shake vigorously for 10 seconds. Empty the ice from the martini glass. Strain the drink into the chilled glass. Garnish with the almond and serve immediately.

# Nutty Manhattan

THIS REVIVAL WILL IMPRESS THE SMART SET WITH ITS
OFF-BROADWAY SENSIBILITIES. ITALIAN WALNUT LIQUEUR
DOES NOT OFTEN FIND ITS NAME IN LIGHTS, BUT AFTER
BOURBON-LOVERS TASTE THIS MELT-IN-YOUR MOUTH
ELIXIR, IT IS SURE TO BECOME THE NEXT SUPERSTAR.

*Serves 1*

**Cocktail ice cubes for chilling and shaking**

**2 ¹/₂ ounces Maker's Mark bourbon**

**¹/₂ ounce Nocello liqueur**

**1 maraschino cherry for garnish**

Fill a 5-ounce martini glass with ice and set aside to chill. Fill a tempered pint glass with ice and add the bourbon and Nocello. Cap the glass with a stainless-steel cocktail shaker and shake vigorously for 10 seconds. Empty the ice from the martini glass. Strain the drink into the chilled glass. Garnish with the cherry and serve immediately.

# Goosey

THE GOOSEY IS AN AROMATIC MARTINI THAT AROUSES
THE HERBACEOUS NOTES OF FRENCH CHARTREUSE
LIQUEUR. THE LIME TWIST BRIGHTENS EACH HERBAL SUG-
GESTION IN THE COCKTAIL FOR AN UNUSUAL MARTINI
WITH A CLEAR GREEN BRILLIANCE.

*Serves* 1

Cocktail ice cubes for
chilling and shaking

1/2 ounce Green
Chartreuse liqueur

3 ounces Grey Goose
vodka

1 lime twist for garnish

Fill a 5-ounce martini glass with ice and set aside to chill for several minutes. Empty the ice from the glass and add the Chartreuse liqueur. Coat the inside of the chilled glass with the Chartreuse by gently rotating the stem of the glass in full circles. Pour out the liqueur. Fill a tempered pint glass with ice and add the vodka. Cap the glass with a stainless-steel cocktail shaker and shake vigorously for 10 seconds. Strain the drink into the martini glass. Garnish with the lime twist and serve immediately.

# Cable

THE CABLE SALUTES CITY SLICKERS WITH A METROPOLITAN
SLANT ON THE STANDARD SIDECAR. RED CURRANT PURÉE
ADDS AN EXTRA-TART JAB THAT ONLY A SEASONED
URBAN DWELLER COULD LOVE.

Serves 1

| | | |
|---|---|---|
| Cocktail ice cubes for shaking | 1/4 ounce Harlequin orange liqueur | 2 tablespoons Red Currant Purée (page 21) |
| 2 1/2 ounces Korbel brandy | 1 ounce Fresh Lemon-Lime Juice (page 20) | Lollipop Rim (page 25) for garnish |
| | 1 ounce Simple Syrup (page 20) | |

Fill a tempered pint glass with ice and add the brandy,
liqueur, lemon-lime juice, simple syrup,
and red currant purée. Cap the glass with
a stainless-steel cocktail shaker and shake
vigorously for 10 seconds. Strain into a
10-ounce martini glass garnished with a
lollipop rim. Serve immediately.

# Blue Margarita

THIS DEMURE DRINK REPLACES THE IMPOSING ZEST OF A MARGARITA WITH THE GENTLE FLORAL BOUQUET OF PARFAIT AMOUR. ETHEREAL ORANGE BLOSSOMS AND ROSES CUSHION THE TEQUILA FOR A COY VERSION OF A SUMMERTIME FAVORITE.

*Serves 1*

| | | |
|---|---|---|
| Cocktail ice cubes for shaking and serving | ³/₄ ounce Parfait Amour liqueur | 1 ounce Simple Syrup (page 20) |
| 1 1/2 ounces Sauza Hornitos tequila | 1 ounce Fresh Lemon-Lime Juice (page 20) | 1 lime wedge |

Fill a tempered pint glass with ice and add the tequila, liqueur, lemon-lime juice, and simple syrup. Cap the glass with a stainless-steel cocktail shaker and shake vigorously for 10 seconds. Pour the drink and ice into a bucket glass. Garnish with the lime wedge. Serve immediately, with a straw.

HIP SIPS

# Lucy's Sidecar

AVOID SCURVY WITH THIS PIRATED VERSION OF THE
TRADITIONAL SIDECAR. IF YOU ARE BUOYANT ENOUGH
TO BE TOSSED ABOUT IN UNCHARTED WATERS WITHOUT
LOSING THE PARROT FROM YOUR SHOULDER, YOU WILL
SOON FIND IT'S NOT SO DIFFICULT TO NAVIGATE BY THE
NORTH STAR WHILE SAVORING THE EQUATORIAL SPICES
OF RUM AND VANILLA.

 *Serves 1*

**Cocktail ice cubes
for shaking**

**2 ounces Captain
Morgan Private Stock
spiced rum**

**¼ ounce Harlequin
orange liqueur**

**1 ounce Fresh Lemon-
Lime Juice (page 20)**

**1 ounce Simple Syrup
(page 20)**

**2 tablespoons Mandarin
Purée (page 22)**

**GARNISH**
**Lollipop Rim (page 25)**

**1 orange slice**

Fill a tempered pint glass with ice and add the rum,
liqueur, lemon-lime juice, simple syrup,
and mandarin purée. Cap the glass with a
stainless-steel cocktail shaker and shake
vigorously for 10 seconds. Strain into a
10-ounce martini glass garnished with a
lollipop rim. Garnish with the orange slice.
Serve immediately.

# Mr. 820

OUR HOUSE MARTINI IS NAMED FOR THE 820 LOUNGE NEXT TO MY RESTAURANT. AS SMOOTH AS A JAMES BOND PROTÉGÉ, MR. 820 WILL SIMULTANEOUSLY SEND YOU RACING DOWN FRENCH PROVINCIAL ROADS AND GET YOU TO REVEAL ALL YOUR SECRETS. DEBONAIR AND FLUENT IN THE LANGUAGE OF LOVE, MR. 820 INVITES YOU TO CAST CAUTION TO THE WIND AND SPEND THE NIGHT WITH A SKILLED SUITOR.

*Serves 1*

**Cocktail ice cubes for chilling and shaking**

**3 ounces Boodles gin**

**5 fresh rosemary leaves, plus 1 rosemary sprig for garnish**

Fill a 5-ounce martini glass with ice and set aside to chill. Fill a tempered pint glass with ice and add the gin and rosemary leaves. Cap the pint glass with a stainless-steel cocktail shaker and shake vigorously for 10 seconds. Empty the ice from the martini glass. Strain the drink into the chilled glass. Garnish with the rosemary sprig. Serve immediately.

# Marco's Bloody Mary

*Serves 1*

NAMED FOR MARCO DIONYSUS, A FELLOW MIXOLOGIST IN SAN FRANCISCO, MARCO'S BLOODY MARY IS A GARDEN IN A GLASS AND A SUPERB REASON TO VISIT THE FARMERS' MARKET TO GATHER INFUSION-WORTHY VEGETABLES FOR BLOODY MARY VODKA. FOR ANOTHER VARIATION, INFUSE TEQUILA WITH THE SAME INGREDIENTS AND SHAKE UP A BLOODY MARIA.

| | | |
|---|---|---|
| Cocktail ice cubes for shaking and serving | Splash of Cerignola olive juice | Dash of celery salt |
| 3 ounces tomato juice | 2 tablespoons Fresh Lemon-Lime Juice (page 20) | **GARNISH** |
| 2 ounces Bloody Mary Vodka (recipe follows) | | Salt rim (page 25) |
| | | 1 asparagus sprig |
| 5 to 6 dashes Worcestershire sauce | 2 teaspoons finely grated fresh horseradish | 1 pickled carrot |
| | | 2 olives |

Fill a tempered pint glass with ice and add the tomato juice, Bloody Mary vodka, Worcestershire sauce, olive juice, lemon-lime juice, horse-radish, and celery salt. Cap the glass with a stainless-steel cocktail shaker and shake vigorously for 10 seconds. Pour the drink and ice into a pint glass garnished with a salt rim. Spear the asparagus, carrot, and olives on a toothpick and add to the drink. Squeeze the juice from the lime wedge over the drink and finish with cracked pepper.

Bloody Mary Vodka Combine the bell peppers, chile, garlic, and basil in a wide-mouthed glass jar with a lid, such as a

1 lime wedge

Freshly cracked pepper to taste

**FOR BLOODY MARY VODKA**

1/4 yellow bell pepper, seeded and cut into thin strips

1/4 red bell pepper, seeded and cut into thin strips

1/4 orange bell pepper, seeded and cut into thin strips

1/2 small jalapeño chile, seeded and minced

1 large garlic clove, sliced

4 fresh basil leaves

1 bottle (1 liter) Monopolowa vodka (see note)

2-gallon storage jar. Add the vodka and seal the container. (Reserve the vodka bottle for refilling.) Store in a cool, dark place for 2 days. Remove the vegetables with a slotted spoon and strain the vodka. Using a funnel, pour the infused vodka back into the reserved vodka bottle. Use now or cap and refrigerate for up to 6 months. Gently shake the vodka before using to distribute any spices that may have settled.

*Makes 1 liter*

*Note: Bloody Maria Tequila* Substitute tequila for the vodka and use in place of Bloody Mary Vodka for a twist on the classic Bloody Mary cocktail.

# Irish Stout Sangría

IN THIS COMFORTING COLD-WEATHER SANGRÍA, THE
BITTER FLAVORS OF STOUT ARE FINE-TUNED WITH SWEET
NOTES OF RUBY PORT. IRISH STOUT SANGRÍA IS A ROBUST
BREW AND A FINE COMPLEMENT TO A POT ROAST OR A
MIDNIGHT ROUND OF FISH AND CHIPS.

*Serves 1*

1 bottle (16 ounces)
Murphy's Irish Stout

¹/₂ ounce Simple Syrup
(page 20)

¹/₂ ounce ruby port

**GARNISH**

Dash of freshly grated
nutmeg

Dash of ground
cinnamon

*In a chilled pint glass, combine 12 ounces of the stout* and the simple syrup. Allow the stout to settle, then add the port. Gently stir 3 times with a bar spoon to mix the ingredients. Top off with the remaining stout and allow the drink to settle for 30 seconds. Garnish with nutmeg and cinnamon. Serve immediately.

# Pisco Sour

AFTER A LONG DAY OF WATCHING WILDLIFE ON THE SHORES OF THE GALÁPAGOS OR HIKING THE RUINS OF MACHU PICCHU, RAISE A TOAST TO EXOTIC LANDS WITH PERU'S SIGNATURE COCKTAIL. THIS VERSION GETS ADDED ZIP FROM MUDDLED LEMON, SUGAR, BITTERS, AND MARASCHINO CHERRIES.

*Serves* 1

1 sugar cube

5 dashes Angostura bitters

1/4 lemon

2 maraschino cherries, stemmed, plus 2 with stems for garnish

Cocktail ice cubes for muddling, shaking, and serving

2 ounces Alto del Carmen Pisco brandy

1 ounce Fresh Lemon-Lime Juice (page 20)

1 ounce Simple Syrup (page 20)

*Put the sugar cube in the bottom of a tempered pint glass* and coat the cube thoroughly with the bitters. Add the lemon wedge, 2 stemmed cherries, and 1/2 cup ice cubes to the glass. Muddle the ingredients thoroughly (see page 15) until the ice is red and slushy. Fill the glass with ice. Add the brandy, lemon-lime juice, and simple syrup. Cap the glass with a stainless-steel cocktail shaker and shake vigorously for 10 seconds. Pour the drink and ice into a bucket glass. Garnish with the 2 cherries with stems and serve immediately.

# Smoky Martini

WITH A SMOKY MARTINI IN HAND, YOU ARE PRIMED TO
WRITE THE NEXT GREAT AMERICAN NOVEL. THE SECRET
TO THIS DRINK IS YOUR PRIZED BOTTLE OF SCOTCH SAFELY
LODGED BETWEEN JAMES AND JOYCE. WHEN THE LIBRARY
WALLS START TO CLOSE IN, CRADLE A SMOKY MARTINI
AND WATCH THE WORDS FLOW.

Serves 1

**Cocktail ice cubes for
chilling and shaking**

**3 ounces gin or vodka**

**¹/₄ ounce single-malt
Scotch whisky**

**1 lemon twist for
garnish**

Fill a 5-ounce martini glass with ice and set aside to
chill. Fill a tempered pint glass with ice and
add the gin or vodka and Scotch. Cap the
glass with a stainless-steel cocktail shaker
and shake vigorously for 10 seconds. Empty
the ice from the martini glass. Strain the
drink into the chilled glass. Garnish with
the lemon twist and serve immediately.

# Mandarin Margarita, a.k.a. House Margarita

*Serves 1*

ALLOW YOUR TRAIN WRECK OF A WORK WEEK TO COME
TO A SCREECHING HALT WITH A MANDARIN MARGARITA.
TEQUILA, MANDARIN PURÉE, SALT, AND LIME WILL
SUFFUSE YOUR BODY WITH RELAXATION AS YOU SLOWLY
UNWIND AND PREPARE TO JETTISON YOUR CELL PHONE.

Cocktail ice cubes for shaking

2 ounces Don Eduardo silver tequila

1/4 ounce Grand Marnier liqueur

1 ounce Fresh Lemon-Lime juice (page 20)

1 ounce Simple Syrup (page 20)

2 tablespoons Mandarin Purée (page 22)

**GARNISH**

Salt rim (page 25)

1 lime slice

1 orange slice

Fill a tempered pint glass with ice and add the tequila,
Grand Marnier, lemon-lime juice, simple
syrup, and mandarin purée. Cap the glass
with a stainless-steel cocktail shaker and
shake vigorously for 10 seconds. Strain into
a 10-ounce martini glass garnished with
a salt rim. Garnish with the lime slice and
orange slice. Serve immediately.

# Sentimental Sips

There is something to be said for a drink that never goes out of style. Sentimental Sips are like ViewMasters of the past: card tables and quick rounds of hearts, your dad sitting in the living room after work, the Christmas parties when you were sent to bed early, your mom with her bouffant hairdo.

A worn liquor cabinet that smells of bourbon brings back memories of when we wanted to be all grown up and share in the secret society that navigated through the world without a hitch.

*Hip Sips* may have come a long way from those days, but these next few drinks got us started.

# Champagne Cocktail

CHAMPAGNE COCKTAILS NEVER GO OUT OF STYLE. THIS
PEPPY DRINK FITS RIGHT IN WITH ANY MENU, FROM
CUCUMBER SANDWICHES TO THANKSGIVING TURKEY.

*Serves 1*

1 sugar cube

4 dashes Angostura
bitters

4 ounces dry
Champagne

1 lemon twist for
garnish

*Put the sugar cube in a 6-ounce Champagne flute.*
Sprinkle all sides of the sugar cube with
the bitters. Add the Champagne gradually
to prevent bubbling over. Garnish with the
lemon twist and serve immediately.

# Moscow Mule

Serves 1

INFORMANTS, WHEN THE TELEPHONE IS TAPPED AND
YOU'VE JUST FOUND OUT YOUR GIRLFRIEND IS A DOUBLE
AGENT, TOSS BACK A MOSCOW MULE. THE EXTRA SPICE
(CODE WORD: *GINGER*) WILL HAVE YOU TUNNELING
BENEATH THE IRON CURTAIN FOR A SECRET RENDEZVOUS
WITH YOUR ATTACHÉ.

| | | |
|---|---|---|
| **Cocktail ice cubes for serving** | **¼ ounce Fresh Lemon-Lime Juice (page 20)** | **1 lemon slice for garnish** |
| **2 ounces Monopolowa vodka** | **3 ounces Reed's ginger beer (see Sources)** | |

Fill a Collins glass with ice. Add the vodka and
lemon juice and stir gently with a
bar spoon. Top off the drink with the
ginger beer. Garnish with the lemon
slice. Serve at once, with a straw.

# Negroni

LAUNCH YOUR VERY OWN ROMAN HOLIDAY WITH
THIS BITTER TONIC. THIS RENOWNED ITALIAN APERITIF
WILL HAVE YOU RACING PAST THE PAPARAZZI ON
YOUR VESPA.

*Serves 1*

**Cocktail ice cubes for chilling and shaking**

**1 ounce gin**

**1 ounce Campari**

**1 ounce sweet vermouth**

**1 orange twist for garnish**

*Fill a 5-ounce martini glass with ice and set aside* to chill. Fill a tempered pint glass with ice and add the gin, Campari, and sweet vermouth. Cap the glass with a stainless-steel cocktail shaker and shake vigorously for 10 seconds. Empty the ice from the martini glass. Strain the drink into the chilled glass. Garnish with the orange twist and serve immediately.

# The Original Lemon Drop

A SHOCKING CHOMP OF A LEMON WEDGE COATED IN
SUGAR IS FOLLOWED BY A SINGLE SHOT OF VODKA IN THIS
MOUTH-PUCKERING, SPINE-TINGLING DRINK.

*Serves 1*

**1 lemon wedge**

**Baker's sugar for coating**

**2 ounces well-chilled Absolut Citron vodka**

Coat both sides of the lemon wedge with a modest amount
of baker's sugar and place on a small plate.
Pour the chilled vodka into a shot glass.
Bite into the lemon wedge, and then drink
the shot.

# Lemon Drop

CITRUS SPIKES THIS SWEET-TART, BREATHTAKING DRINK.
LEMON DROPS WILL LIFT YOU ABOVE THE ACTION LIKE A
PAIR OF JIMMY CHOO STILETTOS.

*Serves 1*

| | | |
|---|---|---|
| Cocktail ice cubes for shaking | 1 ounce Fresh Lemon-Lime Juice (page 20) | **GARNISH**<br>Lollipop Rim (page 25) |
| 2 1/2 ounces Grey Goose Le Citron vodka | 1 ounce Simple Syrup (page 20) | 1 lemon slice |
| 1/4 ounce Cointreau orange liqueur | Splash of fresh orange juice | |

Fill a tempered pint glass with ice and add the vodka, Cointreau, lemon-lime juice, simple syrup, and orange juice. Cap the glass with a stainless-steel cocktail shaker and shake vigorously for 10 seconds. Strain into a 10-ounce martini glass garnished with a lollipop rim and the lemon slice. Serve immediately.

# Manhattan

SYNONYMOUS WITH CIGAR SMOKE, DARK PANELED WALLS,
AND THE BOYS' CLUBS OF NEW YORK CITY, MANHATTANS
ARE ESPECIALLY ENJOYED BY THE BOLD BOURBON
DRINKER WHO DOESN'T SHY AWAY FROM PLATINUM-CARD
LUNCHES OR MERGERS AND ACQUISITIONS.

*Serves 1*

Cocktail ice cubes for chilling and shaking

3 ounces Maker's Mark bourbon

¼ ounce sweet vermouth

2 dashes Angostura bitters

1 maraschino cherry for garnish

Fill a 5-ounce martini glass with ice and set aside to chill. Fill a tempered pint glass with ice and add the bourbon, vermouth, and bitters. Cap the pint glass with a stainless-steel cocktail shaker and shake vigorously for 10 seconds. Empty the ice from the martini glass. Strain the drink into the chilled glass. Garnish with the cherry and serve immediately.

# Rob Roy

IF THE HOTEL RESTAURANT'S GILDED WALLS AND
DINNER MENU HASN'T CHANGED IN FORTY YEARS, ORDER
A ROB ROY. THIS AFFABLE VARIATION ON THE MANHATTAN
IS A HANDSOME COMPANION TO PRIME RIB AU JUS.

Serves 1

Cocktail ice cubes for
chilling and shaking

3 ounces Dewar's
Scotch whisky

Dash of Angostura
bitters

1/4 ounce sweet
vermouth

1 lemon twist or
cherry for garnish

Fill a 5-ounce martini glass with ice and set aside to chill. Fill a tempered pint glass with ice and add the Scotch, bitters, and vermouth. Cap the glass with a stainless-steel cocktail shaker and shake vigorously for 10 seconds. Empty the ice from the martini glass. Strain the drink into the chilled glass. Garnish with the lemon twist or cherry and serve immediately.

# Mai Tai

*Serves* 1

THIS LIQUID VACATION WILL MEET YOU FOR SHUFFLEBOARD ON THE LIDO DECK OR DINNER AT THE CAPTAIN'S TABLE. THE ONLY THING THAT STANDS IN THE WAY OF THIS DRINK AND TRUE LOVE IS THE BLINDING GLARE REFLECTING FROM CAPTAIN STUBING'S HEAD.

Cocktail ice cubes for shaking and serving

2 ounces aged rum

1/4 ounce Harlequin orange liqueur

1 ounce Fresh Lemon-Lime Juice (page 20)

1 ounce Simple Syrup (page 20)

1 ounce pineapple juice

1/4 ounce grenadine syrup

1/4 ounce orgeat syrup (see Sources)

GARNISH

1 lime slice

1 mint sprig

Fill a tempered pint glass with ice and add the rum, liqueur, lemon-lime juice, simple syrup, grenadine, and orgeat syrup. Cap the glass with a stainless-steel cocktail shaker and shake vigorously for 10 seconds. Pour the drink and ice into a balloon wineglass. Garnish with the lime slice and mint. Serve immediately.

# Mojito

BARSTOOL-TRAVEL TO A CITY WHERE CIGAR SMOKE PERFUMES THE AIR AND CLUBS BUSTLE WITH MUSIC AND DANCING. WHEN THE SUN CROSSES THE HORIZON, THE MOJITO IS YOUR RESPITE FROM A HOT, HUMID HAVANA NIGHT.

*Serves 1*

**Cocktail ice cubes for shaking and serving**

**5 fresh mint leaves**

**2 ounces Bacardi silver rum**

**1 ounce Fresh Lemon-Lime Juice (page 20)**

**1 ounce Simple Syrup (page 20)**

**Splash of soda water**

**1 mint sprig**

Fill a tempered pint glass one-fourth full with ice cubes and add the mint leaves. Add ice to fill the glass. Add the rum, lemon-lime juice, and simple syrup. Cap the glass with a stainless-steel cocktail shaker and shake vigorously for 10 seconds to bruise the mint leaves and thoroughly mix the ingredients. Pour the drink and ice into a Collins glass and top off with the soda water. Garnish with the mint and serve with 2 straws.

# Sazerac

IF LIFE IS A CABARET, THE SAZERAC IS ONE OF
THE HOUSE DRINKS. PUT ON YOUR BEADS AND LET
THIS NEW ORLEANS SPECIALTY BRING A LITTLE
MARDI GRAS INTO YOUR LIFE.

Cocktail ice cubes for
chilling, muddling, and
shaking

1/2 ounce Pernod liqueur

1 sugar cube

3 dashes Peychaud's
aromatic bitters

3 ounces rye whiskey

1 lemon twist for
garnish

Fill a 5-ounce martini glass with ice and set aside
several minutes to chill. Empty the ice from
the glass and add the Pernod. Coat the
inside of the glass with the Pernod by gently
rotating the stem of the glass in full circles.
Empty the liqueur from the glass.

Put the sugar cube in a tempered pint glass
and coat the cube thoroughly with the bitters.
Cover with 1/2 cup ice. Muddle the ingredients thoroughly (see page 15) until the ice
is slushy. Fill the glass with ice and add the
rye whiskey. Cap the glass with a stainless-
steel cocktail shaker and shake vigorously
for 10 seconds. Strain the drink into the
martini glass. Garnish with the lemon twist
and serve immediately.

# Rusty Nail

SCOTCH GETS A TOUCH OF SWEETNESS
IN THIS TIMELESS COCKTAIL.

*Serves 1*

| Cocktail ice cubes for serving | 2 ½ ounces Dewar's Scotch whisky | ½ ounce Drambuie liqueur |
|---|---|---|

Fill a bucket glass with ice and add the Scotch.
Top off with the Drambuie and
gently stir with a bar spoon to mix
the drink. Serve immediately.

# Tom Collins

THIS DRINK STRIPS AWAY EXCESS FOR A CRISP,
UNDERSTATED REFRESHMENT.

*Serves 1*

| | | |
|---|---|---|
| Cocktail ice cubes for serving | 1 ounce Fresh Lemon-Lime Juice (page 20) | **GARNISH** |
| 2 ounces gin | 1 ounce Simple Syrup (page 20) | 1 lemon slice |
| | Splash of soda water | 2 maraschino cherries |

Fill a Collins glass with ice. Add the gin, lemon-lime juice, and simple syrup. Top off with soda water. Garnish with the lemon slices and cherries. Serve immediately.

# Pimm's Cup

A CLASSIC SUMMERTIME SIP, PIMM'S CUP IS A WELCOME
REFRESHMENT ON A HOT AUGUST AFTERNOON.

*Serves 1*

| | | |
|---|---|---|
| Cocktail ice cubes for serving | 1 ounce Fresh Lemon-Lime Juice (page 20) | Splash of soda water |
| 1 1/2 ounces Pimm's No. 1 | 1 ounce Simple Syrup (page 20) | 1 cucumber slice for garnish |

Fill a Collins glass with ice and add the Pimm's,
lemon-lime juice, and simple syrup.
Top off with soda water. Garnish with the
cucumber slice and serve with a straw.

# Sidecar

THE ORIGINAL GANGSTER OF COCKTAILS, THE SIDECAR
DOESN'T TAKE ANY LIP FROM WANNABE BONNIES AND
CLYDES AND WILL CONFIDENTLY SAUNTER UP TO TONY
SOPRANO AND TELL HIM TO UP HIS DOSAGE.

*Serves 1*

Cocktail ice cubes for
shaking

2 1/2 ounces Korbel
brandy

1/4 ounce Cointreau
orange liqueur

1 ounce Fresh Lemon-
Lime Juice (page 20)

1 ounce Simple Syrup
(page 20)

**GARNISH**

Lollipop Rim
(page 25)

1 lime wedge

Fill a tempered pint glass with ice and add the brandy,
Cointreau, lemon-lime juice, and simple
syrup. Cap the glass with a stainless-steel
cocktail shaker and shake vigorously for
10 seconds. Strain into a 10-ounce martini
glass garnished with a lollipop rim and the
lime wedge. Serve immediately.

# Mint Julep

THE LAND OF CICADAS, CLAY SOIL, AND AFTERNOON THUNDERSTORMS MAY BE WHERE THE MINT JULEP GOT ITS START, BUT ITS MIGRATION ACROSS THE COUNTRY PROVES THAT SOUTHERN COMFORT IS NOT LIMITED TO FRIED CHICKEN AND TURNIP GREENS. YOU CAN SWEET-TALK YOUR WAY OUT OF ALMOST ANY SITUATION WITH ONE OF THESE LIBATIONS.

*Serves 1*

| | | |
|---|---|---|
| **Cocktail ice cubes for shaking and serving** | **2 ounces Maker's Mark bourbon** | **1 ounce Simple Syrup (page 20)** |
| **5 fresh mint leaves, plus 1 mint sprig for garnish** | **1 ounce Fresh Lemon-Lime Juice (page 20)** | **Splash of soda water** |

*Fill a tempered pint glass one-fourth full with ice cubes* and add the mint leaves. Add ice to fill the glass. Add the bourbon, lemon-lime juice, and simple syrup. Cap the glass with a stainless-steel cocktail shaker and shake vigorously for 10 seconds to bruise the mint leaves and thoroughly mix the ingredients. Pour the drink and ice into a bucket glass and top off the drink with soda water. Garnish with the mint and serve at once, with a straw.

# The Classic Martini

A MARTINI MAY BE CLASSIC,
BUT NEVER IS IT RESTRAINED.

Serves 1

**Cocktail ice cubes for chilling and shaking**

**3 ounces Boodles gin**

**2 dashes dry vermouth**

**1 pimento-stuffed green olive**

Fill a 5-ounce martini glass with ice and set aside to chill. Fill a tempered pint glass with ice and add the gin and vermouth. Cap the glass with a stainless-steel cocktail shaker and shake vigorously for 10 seconds. Empty the ice from the martini glass. Strain the drink into the chilled glass, add the olive, and serve at once.

Variation: Replace the gin with vodka. Garnish by running a lemon twist or a grapefruit twist around the rim of the glass and drop the twist into the drink. For a Gibson, garnish the drink with a cocktail onion.

# Margarita

SANDY BEACHES AND PALAPAS ARE NOT COMPLETE WITHOUT THIS SALTY COMPANION. WHEN BAJA CALLS WHILE YOU'RE SURFING THE INTERNET, SHAKE UP A MARGARITA AND MULTITASK MAÑANA.

*Serves* 1

| | | |
|---|---|---|
| Cocktail ice cubes for shaking and serving | 1 ounce Fresh Lemon-Lime juice (page 20) | **GARNISH**<br>Salt Rim (page 25) |
| 2 ounces Sauza Hornitos tequila | 1 ounce Simple Syrup (page 20) | 1 lime wedge |
| $1/4$ ounce Patrón Citronge orange liqueur | | |

Fill a tempered pint glass with ice and add the tequila, liqueur, lemon-lime juice, and simple syrup. Cap the glass with a stainless-steel cocktail shaker and shake vigorously for 10 seconds. Pour the drink and ice into a bucket glass garnished with a salt rim. Add additional ice if necessary to fill the glass. Garnish with the lime wedge. Serve immediately.

# Kamikaze

THE KAMIKAZE IS THE HUMBLE FOUNDATION FOR
MANY MODERN COCKTAILS, INCLUDING THE LEMON
DROP AND COSMOPOLITAN. MUDDLED FRESH LIME AND
SUGAR CUBES ADD CLEAR SWEET-AND-SOUR NOTES
TO THIS COCKTAIL.

*Serves 1*

| | | |
|---|---|---|
| Cocktail ice cubes for chilling and shaking | 2 1/2 ounces Monopolowa vodka | 1/4 ounce Simple Syrup (page 20) |
| 2 sugar cubes | 1/4 ounce Fresh Lemon-Lime Juice (page 20) | |
| 2 lime wedges | | |

Fill a 5-ounce martini glass with ice and set aside to chill. Put the sugar cubes in a tempered pint glass, add 1/2 cup ice, and place 1 lime wedge on top of the ice. Muddle the ingredients thoroughly (see page 15) until the ice is slushy. Fill the glass with ice. Add the vodka, lemon-lime juice, and simple syrup. Cap the glass with a stainless-steel cocktail shaker and shake vigorously for 10 seconds. Empty the ice from the martini glass. Strain the drink into the chilled glass. Garnish with the other lime wedge and serve immediately.

# Old-Fashioned

HERE'S A WAY TO MAKE GRANDPA HAPPIER THAN WATCHING THE RED SOX WIN. A HANDCRAFTED OLD-FASHIONED WILL HAVE HIM REMINISCING ABOUT AVA GARDNER AND PENNANT GAMES AGAINST THE YANKEES.

*Serves 1*

1 sugar cube

5 dashes Angostura bitters

1 maraschino cherry, stemmed

1 orange wedge

Cocktail ice cubes for muddling and serving

2 ounces Maker's Mark bourbon

2 ounces soda water

**GARNISH**

1 maraschino cherry

1 orange slice

Put the sugar cube in a tempered pint glass and coat the sugar cube with the bitters. Add the cherry, orange wedge, and 1/2 cup ice. Muddle the ingredients thoroughly (see page 15) until the ice is slushy. Fill the glass with ice. Add the Maker's Mark. Cap the glass with a stainless-steel cocktail shaker and shake vigorously for 10 seconds. Pour the drink and ice into a bucket glass. Top with additional ice if necessary and add the soda water. Garnish with the cherry and orange slice. Serve immediately.

# Irish Coffee

IF YOU'VE NEVER KISSED THE BLARNEY STONE, YOU
MIGHT NOT HAVE THE GIFT OF GAB, BUT ONE KISS OF
AN IRISH COFFEE WILL HAVE YOU SINGING ABOUT
LEPRECHAUNS AND POTS OF GOLD.

Serves 1

1 sugar cube

2 ounces Bushmills
Irish whiskey

3 ounces strong
hot coffee

2 tablespoons Vanilla
Whipped Cream
(page 53) for garnish

Fill a footed coffee mug with hot water and let the glass
heat thoroughly. Pour out the hot water and
put the sugar cube in the glass. Add the
Bushmills and coffee. Dollop the whipped
cream on top of the drink. Lay 2 straws
across the top of the drink and serve at once.

# Mocktails

With your Hip Sips cocktail repertoire complete, it is time to introduce you to a few of my favorite nonalcoholic drinks. The fruit-infused thirst quenchers in this chapter will prove that Hip Sips are not exclusively spirit-filled beverages. The mocktails presented here are similarly inspired by fresh ingredients and have the same zest as a Hip Sips cocktail.

As invigorating alternatives to soda pop, the following drinks combine favorite fruit flavors into refreshments capturing the enthusiasm of a well-made cocktail. Each *sparkling sip* will cheer you through rained-out barbecues, energize sleepy weekend afternoons, or put the sizzle in a Scrabble party.

# Melonade

MELONADE HELPS YOU TO REMINISCE ABOUT THE DAYS
WHEN A BRAND-NEW AVOCADO FRIGIDAIRE WAS THE
BEST THING SINCE SLICED WONDER BREAD.

*Serves 1*

| | | |
|---|---|---|
| Cocktail ice cubes for shaking and serving | 2 tablespoons Melon Purée (page 21) | Lollipop Rim (page 25) for garnish |
| 2 ounces Fresh Lemon-Lime Juice (page 20) | Splash of cranberry juice | 1 cherry for garnish |
| 2 ounces Simple Syrup (page 20) | Splash of soda water | |

Fill a tempered pint glass with ice and add the lemon-lime juice, simple syrup, melon purée, and cranberry juice. Cap the glass with a stainless-steel cocktail shaker and shake vigorously for 10 seconds. Pour the drink and ice into a pint glass garnished with a lollipop rim. Top off the drink with soda water and add additional ice if necessary to fill the glass. Garnish with the cherry and serve immediately.

# Passionade

Serves 1

PASSIONADE IS ALL THE JUICE YOU NEED TO CONFIDENTLY ASK OUT YOUR CRUSH OR CORNER YOUR BOSS FOR A RAISE. BOLD AND BRASSY, THIS MOCKTAIL WILL BOLSTER THE TIMID AND DARE THE SHY TO LEAP INTO UNCHARTED TERRITORY.

Cocktail ice cubes for shaking and serving

2 ounces Fresh Lemon-Lime Juice (page 20)

2 ounces Simple Syrup (page 20)

2 tablespoons Passion Fruit Purée (page 23)

Splash of soda water

Lollipop Rim (page 25) for garnish

1 orange slice or lime wedge for garnish

Fill a tempered pint glass with ice and add the lemon-lime juice, simple syrup, and passion fruit purée. Cap the glass with a stainless-steel cocktail shaker and shake vigorously for 10 seconds. Pour the drink and ice into a pint glass garnished with a lollipop rim. Top off the drink with soda water and add additional ice if necessary to fill the glass. Garnish with the orange slice or lime wedge and serve immediately.

# Pineapple Mandarin Dream

THE SPRINKLER SALSAS ACROSS THE LAWN AND
THE ZINNIAS IN THE GARDEN ARE SMILING BACK AT
YOU. PINEAPPLE MANDARIN DREAMS ARE MADE FOR
SEDUCTIVE SUMMER AFTERNOONS SITTING IN THE
SHADE ON THE FRONT-PORCH GLIDER.

Serves 1

Cocktail ice cubes for shaking and serving

2 ounces Fresh Lemon-Lime Juice (page 20)

2 ounces Simple Syrup (page 20)

$1/2$ ounce pineapple juice

1 tablespoon Mandarin Purée (page 22)

Splash of soda water

Lollipop Rim (page 25) for garnish

1 orange or pineapple slice for garnish

Fill a tempered pint glass with ice and add the lemon-lime juice, simple syrup, pineapple juice, and mandarin purée. Cap the glass with a stainless-steel cocktail shaker and shake vigorously for 10 seconds. Pour the drink and ice into a pint glass garnished with a lollipop rim. Top off the drink with soda water and add additional ice if necessary to fill the glass. Garnish with the orange or pineapple slice and serve immediately.

# Sources

### Bendistillery
1470 NE First Street, Suite 800
Bend, Oregon 97701
541-310-0200
www.bendistillery.com
Cascade Mountain gin, Crater Lake
vodka, and hazelnut espresso vodka.

### Monin
2100 Range Road
Clearwater, FL 33765
727-421-3033
www.monin.com
Monin orgeat and vanilla syrups.

### L'Epicerie
P.O. Box 310119
Brooklyn, NY 11231
866-350-7575
www.lepicerie.com
Les Vergers Boiron frozen fruit
purées.

### Perfect Purée
Hayward Enterprises
2700 Napa Valley Corporate Drive,
Suite L
Napa, CA 94558
800-556-3707
www.perfectpurée.com
Frozen fruit purées.

### Reed's
13000 South Spring Street
Los Angeles, CA 90061
800-997-3337
www.reedsgingerbrew.com
Reed's ginger beer.

### Sadaf
Soofer Company
2828 South Alameda Street
Los Angeles, CA 90058
800-852-4050
www.sadaf.com
Pomegranate paste.

### Santa Cruz Organic
P.O. Box 369
Chico, CA 95927
530-899-5010
www.santacruz.com
Lime and lemon juices.

128

# Acknowledgments

Absolut Citron vodka is a registered trademark of V&S Vin and Spirit Aktiebolag (Publ); Absolut Vanilla vodka is a registered trademark of V&S Vin and Spirit Aktiebolag (Publ); Alto del Carmen brandy is a registered trademark of Cooperativa Agricola Pisquera Elqui Limitada; Angostura bitters is a registered trademark of Angostura International; Bacardi rum is a registered trademark of Bacardi & Company Limited; Barbancourt Three Star rum is a registered trademark of Societe du Rhum Barboncourt; Beamish stout is a registered trademark of Beamish & Crawford PLC; Bella di Cerignola preserved olives is a registered trademark of Bioconserve S. R. L.; Boodles gin is a registered trademark of Joseph E. Seagram & Sons, Inc.; Bushmills Irish whiskey is a registered trademark of "Old Bushmills" Distillery Co. Limited; Campari is a registered trademark of Davide Campari Milano S.P.A.; Captain Morgan rum is a registered trademark of Diageo North America, Inc.; Carlos I brandy is a registered trademark of Pedro Domecq, S.A.; Cascade Mountain gin is a registered trademark of Bendistillery; Ciroc Vodka is a registered trademark of Diageo North America, Inc.; Citronge liqueurs is a registered trademark of Caribbean Distillers Corporation, Limited; Cointreau liqueur is a registered trademark of Cointreau Corp.; Cruzan banana rum is a registered trademark of Virgin Islands Rum Industries, Ltd.; Cruzan mango rum is a registered trademark of Virgin Islands Rum Industries, Ltd.; Cruzan orange rum is a registered trademark of Virgin Islands Rum Industries, Ltd.; Cruzan pineapple rum is a registered trademark of Virgin Islands Rum Industries, Ltd.; Cruzan vanilla rum is a registered trademark of Virgin Islands Rum Industries, Ltd.; Dewar's Blended Scotch whiskey is a registered trademark of Bacardi & Company Limited; Don Eduardo tequila is a registered trademark of Tequila Orendain de Jalisco, S.A. de C.V.; Drambuie liqueur is a registered trademark of The Drambuie Liqueur Co., Ltd.; Frangelico liqueur is a registered trademark of Giorgio Barbero and Figli, S.P.A.; Glenmorangie scotch whisky is a registered trademark of Macdonald & Muir Limited; Grand Marnier is a registered trademark of Societe des Produits Marnier-Lapostolle; Chartreuse liqueur is a registered trademark of Chartreuse Corp.; Grey Goose vodka is a registered trademark of Bacardi & Company Limited; Hangar One vodka is a registered trademark of Distillers Art, Inc.; Harlequin orange liqueur is a registered trademark of Kentucky Brands of California, Inc.; Hendrick's gin is a registered trademark of William Grant & Sons, Inc.; Johnnie Walker Scotch whisky is a registered trademark of Johnnie Walker Co.; Kahlúa liqueur is a registered trademark of The Kahlua Co.; Korbel brandy is a registered trademark of F. Korbel and Bros.; The Macallan Scotch whisky is a registered trademark of The Macallan Distillers Ltd.; Maker's Mark bourbon is a registered trademark of Maker's Mark Distillery Inc.; Monopolowa vodka is a registered trademark of Mutual Wholesale Liquor Inc.; Nocello liqueur is a registered trademark of Toschi Vignola S.R.L.; Pampero rum is a registered trademark of Industrias Pampero C.A.; Parfait Amour liqueur is a registered trademark of Marie Brizard & Roger International; Pernod liqueur is a registered trademark of Pernod Ricard; Pimm's No. 1 liqueur is a registered trademark of The Pimm's Company; Pyrat Pistol rum is a registered trademark of Anguilla Rums Limited; Reed's ginger beer is a registered trademark of Original Beverage Corporation; Saint Brendan's Irish Cream liqueur is a registered trademark of Saint Brendan's Irish Cream Liqueur Co. Ltd.; Santa Cruz Organic is a registered trademark of Smucker Quality Beverages, Inc.; Sauza Hornitos tequila is a registered trademark of Tequila Sauza S. A. de C.V.; Smirnoff apple vodka is a registered trademark of Diageo North America, Inc.; Tabasco Sauce hot sauce is a registered trademark of McIlhenny Co.; Tanqueray dry gin is a registered trademark of Gordon's Dry Gin Company, Limited, The; Tia Maria liqueur is a registered trademark of Tia Maria Limited; Tuaca brandy is a registered trademark of Distillerie Tuoni and Canepa S.P.A.

# Index

# Liquid Measurements

| | |
|---|---|
| Bar spoon = | $1/2$ ounce |
| 1 teaspoon = | $1/6$ ounce |
| 1 tablespoon = | $1/2$ ounce |
| 2 tablespoons (pony) = | 1 ounce |
| 3 tablespoons (jigger) = | $1\,1/2$ ounces |
| $1/4$ cup = | 2 ounces |
| $1/3$ cup = | 3 ounces |
| $1/2$ cup = | 4 ounces |
| $2/3$ cup = | 5 ounces |
| $3/4$ cup = | 6 ounces |
| 1 cup = | 8 ounces |
| 1 pint = | 16 ounces |
| 1 quart = | 32 ounces |
| 750 ml bottle = | 25.4 ounces |
| 1 liter bottle = | 33.8 ounces |
| 1 medium lemon = | 3 tablespoons juice |
| 1 medium lime = | 2 tablespoons juice |
| 1 medum orange = | $1/3$ cup juice |